TEST
YOUR
CHRISTIAN
LITERACY

TEST YOUR
YOUR
CHRISTIAN
LITERACY

*What Every Christian
Needs to Know*

Judith A. Lunsford

Wolgemuth & Hyatt, Publishers, Inc.
Brentwood, Tennessee

The mission of Wolgemuth & Hyatt, Publishers, Inc., is to publish and distribute books that lead individuals toward:

- A personal faith in the one true God: Father, Son, and Holy Spirit;

- A lifestyle of practical discipleship; and

- A worldview that is consistent with the historic, Christian faith.

Moreover, the Company endeavors to accomplish this mission at a reasonable profit and in a manner which glorifies God and serves His Kingdom.

Wolgemuth & Hyatt, Publishers, Inc.
1749 Mallory Lane, Suite 110, Brentwood, Tennessee 37027.
Printed in the United States of America.

Library of Congress Cataloging-in-Publication Data

Lunsford, Judith A.
    Test your Christian literacy : what every Christian needs to know / Judith A. Lunsford.
        p. cm.
    ISBN 0-943497-64-7 : $10.95
    1. Bible—Miscellanea. 2. Christianity—Miscellanea. I. Title.
II. Title: Christian literacy.
BS538.L85 1989
200—dc20   89-27740
                                                                  CIP

To Gary, a modern day Barnabas

CONTENTS

ACKNOWLEDGMENTS

No one produces a book alone. While one person may put words to paper (or disk), there are many who contribute in less visible ways. Bill and Linda Pruett, seasoned Bible readers, provided insight in the early stages of this project. Bob Cleveland offered encouragement and counsel at a pivotal phase. Dave Stout, my pastor, graciously lent his reference books and donated the "ships in the fog" story.

I am also grateful to Dr. Max Anders, whose book, *30 Days to Understanding the Bible,* was the springboard for *Test Your Christian Literacy.* Max's zeal for teaching and his respectful handling of the Scriptures have been a personal inspiration.

Special thanks go to my sister, Debra Zandrew, who good-naturedly answered many of the questions in this book and proved the proverb: "Like apples of gold in settings of silver is a word spoken in right circumstances."

The most crucial contributor has been my husband, Gary, who saw the book finished from its inception and whose "vision" pulled me through the mire of countless revisions. He not only read manuscripts, he gallantly rescued me from the throes of a wild mouse, a skewed monitor, mysterious "glitches," and other realites of our computer age.

I am particularly grateful for the discipline this project has imposed in my own life. Joining Jeremiah, I can affirm that the Lord's "compassions never fail."

INTRODUCTION

NEARLY TWO THOUSAND YEARS AGO, Jesus stood on a mountain and said, "Go therefore and make disciples of all the nations, baptizing them in the name of the Father and of the Son and of the Holy Spirit, teaching them to observe all that I commanded you." With these words from the Great Commission, Christ sent the disciples out. What they did has affected the world and each of us.

We who call ourselves "Christians" approach another pinnacle — the twenty-first century. Who are we?

We who name the name of Christ are really not that much different from the New Testament "saints" of two thousand years ago. We share the heritage of Peter, Stephen, and Lydia. We are redeemed sinners who cling to the Scriptures and live out our lives in local churches.

However, in another sense, we are very different from our New Testament brethren. We are products of two thousand years of history. Councils, creeds, schisms, wars, revivals, and renewal have washed over us, making us distinct from the church at Jerusalem or Ephesus or Corinth.

Christians who peer at the twenty-first century possess a dual heritage: a legacy of Scripture and a legacy of dynamic faith. Most of us sample this rich and complex heritage in delicate bites. We nibble our way through Proverbs or munch a devotional or snack on a gospel. Sometimes, we gnaw on a Christian biography or gulp a missionary film. These activities contribute to our spiritual awareness, but they focus on only a part of our Christian heritage.

As a result, we are Christians with spiritual myopia. We see a few fixed fields, like missions or evangelism, but squint at subjects, like poetry or prophecy, that are beyond our range of interest. We seldom synthesize the diverse components of our Christian heritage to form a meaningful whole.

If Christ returned today and walked the streets of Chattanooga, Poughkeepsie, or Fresno, what would He discover as He talked with Christians He met? Would He find us knowledgeable witnesses for our faith? Would He find us at least literate?

Literacy is the ability to think and communicate about a subject with competence. An emphasis on "cultural literacy" has recently sent Americans scrambling to remember what they learned in high school. But Christian literacy is not just a hedge against personal embarrassment; rather, it is an investment in the future.

Christ's instruction in Matthew 28:19–20 was to teach new disciples to observe all that He commanded. The new disciples, in turn, would mature and teach others. The modern day teacher who barely knows Peter from Paul, Hebrews from Malachi, or Samaria from Judea, has little substance to transmit.

What is it that modern believers should know? What are the basics of Christianity?

Test Your Christian Literacy is a tool for understanding the basics of our Christian heritage. Part I highlights the major divisions of the Bible: geography, general information, Old Testament history, poetical books, prophetical books, New Testament history, the epistles, and Bible personalities.

Part II covers the post-New Testament period and includes doctrine, church history, pivotal people, and the modern missionary movement. Each chapter consists of an introduction and a fifty-question test, followed immediately by an answer section.

The questions selected test observation, recall, or understanding. They are not trivia. The questions are basic. They cause us to think about the Christian concepts and phrases we frequently hear and take for granted.

The answers are designed to challenge our understanding and quickly tie it to Scripture or history. Some of the answers will give us insight, some will impart knowledge, and one or two will, we hope, provide a laugh. Scripture references have been included as an integral part of the answer; they substantiate conclusions and provide opportunities for further study.

The chapter divisions set forth the basic areas of Christianity and help us quickly (and privately) discover where our strengths and weaknesses lie. Areas of our Christian literacy that need improvement may be addressed by using the Suggested Reading List at the back of the book.

Test Your Christian Literacy may be used randomly, with the reader digging into those sections that delight or challenge; or the book may be used systematically, moving from geography through missions. Generally, readers will derive the greatest benefit from the systematic approach.

Two and one-half centuries ago Jonathan Edwards wrote: "That religion which God requires, and will accept, does not consist in weak, dull, and lifeless wishes, raising us but a little above a state of indifference. God, in his word, greatly insists upon it, that we be in good earnest, fervent in spirit, and our hearts vigorously engaged in religion."

Whether we Christians enter the twenty-first century in indifference or spiritual vigor is largely dependent on us.

Scoring

Each question is worth two points. Tally your score and record it on the chart on the next page. The graph will indicate your progress.

90 – 100	Excellent!
80 – 88	Above average
70 – 78	Fair
60 and below	See "Suggested Reading List"

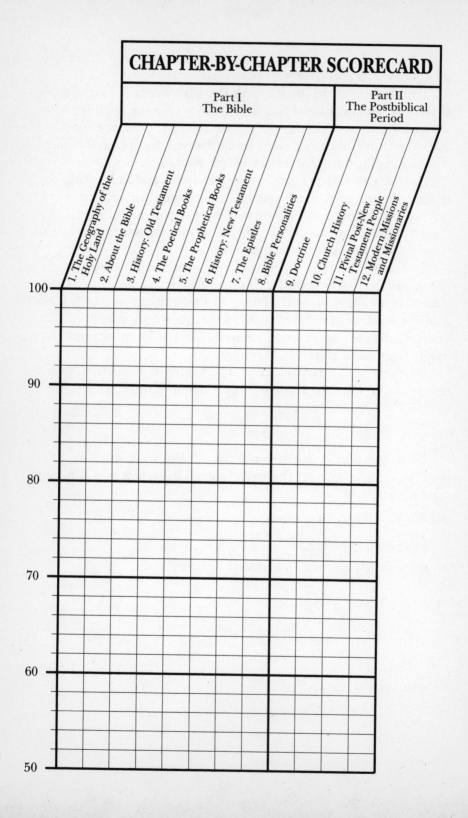

PART ONE

THE BIBLE

ONE

THE GEOGRAPHY OF THE HOLY LAND

IT'S NOT OFTEN THAT A TEACHER becomes a media sensation by merely giving a quiz. But Dr. David Helgren of the University of Miami did.

In the mid-1980s, the results of Dr. Helgren's quiz made the nightly news, "Good Morning, America," and scores of newspapers and journals. His test revealed that American college students, busily carving careers, manning their computers, and scaling academic heights, had become ignorant of the world around them. Their "geographical astuteness level" was at an all-time low, and their trouble wasn't just with Namibia or Timor.

Seven percent of the students tested, sitting in a classroom in Miami, Florida, could not locate Miami on the map in front of them. Twenty percent could not find New York City. One-third could not locate the Pacific Ocean.

Disbelieving educators, journalists, and pollsters repeated the test with a wider audience. Their results? Basically the same. Adults, as a whole, do not know much about geography.

What is this subject Americans ignore? Just what is geography?

Geography is the study that deals with the earth and its life forms: mountains, rivers, resources, people, and climate. Geography helps us absorb information about our environment and respond in practical ways. Are you headed for Kauai, Hawaii? Pack an umbrella. It's the rainiest spot in America. Are you

7

hungry in Belize? Skip the "bamboo chicken" or you'll dine on iguana!

From an eternal perspective, it may not matter whether a Christian finds his way to Upper Volta, pinpoints Brasilia, or prepares adequately for Sahel, but the believer who habitually ignores the world around him will probably have very little appreciation for the geography of the Bible.

According to a recent study by the Barna Research Group of Glendale, California, nearly one-quarter of the people who call themselves born-again Christians never read the Bible. This fact reveals an atmosphere of Biblical ignorance.

"Many Christians do not even know things such as where Jesus was born," reported George Barna, president of Barna Research. "If they are uninformed about elementary things . . . , how can they be expected to intelligently discuss the content of the Scriptures with an unbeliever or to live in a manner consistent with Biblical principles?"

The gospel simply cannot be separated from its geography. Jesus dwelt on earth. He was killed according to the customs of men. His Resurrection was punctuated by earthquakes and confirmed by Cleopas near Emmaus and the apostles in Jerusalem. It is not simply hard to tell the "old, old story" without geography—it is impossible! Galilee, the Jordan, and a mere hill called Calvary—an understanding of what happened at these important pieces of earth forks—the road between heaven and hell.

As Mr. Barna indicated, geography is "elementary." So, it is here that we begin.

Questions

1. On the next page is a map of the Holy Land. Egypt is the section of the map labeled

   a.   b.   c.   d.

2. Assyria is the section of the map labeled

   a.   b.   c.   d.

Locations of the Old Testament

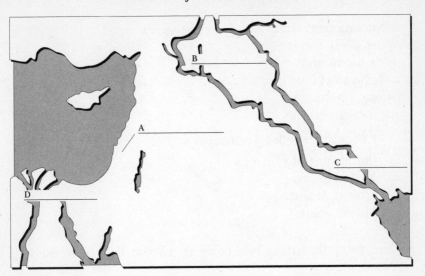

3. Persia is the section of the map labeled
   a.   b.   c.   d.

4. The patriarchs earned their living as
   a. farmers.
   b. tradesmen.
   c. craftsmen.
   d. keepers of cattle.

5. Moses received the Ten Commandments on
   a. Mount Nebo.
   b. Mount of Olives.
   c. Mount Gerizim.
   d. Mount Sinai.

6. Food that would never have appeared on David's royal menu was
   a. roasted quail.
   b. venison stew.
   c. ham sandwiches.

   d. grilled fish.

7. The nation of Israel has ___ time zones.
   a. one.
   b. two.
   c. three.
   d. four.

8. The building site for Jerusalem was
   a. the Mount of Olives.
   b. Mount Sinai.
   c. Mount Ararat.
   d. Mount Zion.

9. The term that does not refer to all the land promised to Abraham is
   a. the Negev.
   b. Canaan.
   c. the Promised Land.
   d. Israel.

10. Jerusalem is located in the
    a. Coastal Plain.
    b. Transjordan.
    c. Western Plateau or Hill Country.
    d. Jordan Valley or Jordan Rift.

11. Jacob met Rachel, Eliezer met Rebekah, and Moses met Zipporah near a
    a. mountain.
    b. well.
    c. copper mine.
    d. forest.

12. The general climate of Israel most closely parallels that of the U.S. at
    a. Seattle, Washington.

b. Boston, Massachusetts.

c. Palm Springs, California.

d. Kauai, Hawaii.

13. Eden was

a. Abraham's hometown.

b. a garden in Mesopotamia.

c. an altar in Canaan.

d. Ishmael's eventual homeland.

14. From "Dan to Beersheba," a phrase referring to Israel's north to south borders, is a distance of approximately

a. 25 miles.

b. 75 miles.

c. 150 miles.

d. 350 miles.

15. Below is another map of the Holy Land. The Mediterranean Sea is the section of the map labeled

a. b. c. d.

Bodies of Water of the Old Testament

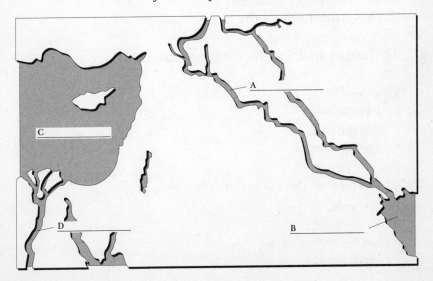

16. The Nile is the section of the map labeled

 a.   b.   c.   d.

17. The Euphrates is the section of the map labeled

 a.   b.   c.   d.

18. Joshua led the Israelites into the Promised Land through
 a. Gaza.
 b. Beersheba.
 c. Gilgal.
 d. Dan.

19. The mountain where Noah's ark rested was
 a. Ararat.
 b. Carmel.
 c. Ebal.
 d. Moriah.

20. The land of Goshen is
 a. in the heart of the Sinai.
 b. the northeastern part of the Nile Delta.
 c. the suburbs of Nineveh.
 d. the eastern side of the Sea of Galilee.

21. The burial spot for the patriarchs and three of their wives was
 a. a cave.
 b. a palm tree.
 c. a river bed.
 d. an oak tree.

22. The capital of the nation of Israel was
 a. Hebron.
 b. Bethlehem.
 c. Bethel.
 d. Jerusalem.

23. An animal associated with Judah, Samson, and Daniel is

    a. the sparrow.
    b. the eagle.
    c. the lion.
    d. the fox.

24. The nation that most frequently attacked King Solomon was

    a. Egypt.
    b. Moab.
    c. Philistia.
    d. none of the above.

25. Fellow exiles Daniel and Ezekiel lived and wrote in

    a. Jerusalem.
    b. Damascus.
    c. Babylon.
    d. Samaria.

26. The tabernacle in the wilderness was

    a. the high priest's home.
    b. a tent for worship.
    c. one of Abraham's wells.
    d. a box for the Ten Commandments, Aaron's rod, and manna.

27. Fauna not involved in the plagues on Egypt were

    a. quail.
    b. lice or gnats.
    c. frogs.
    d. livestock.

28. On the next page is another map of the Holy Land. The Dead Sea is the section of the map labeled

    a.   b.   c.   d.

Bodies of Water of the Old Testament

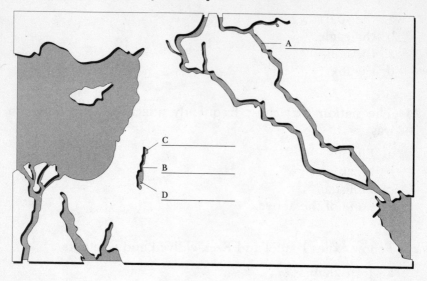

29. The Jordan River is the section of the map labeled

    a.   b.   c.   d.

30. *Denarius*, *drachma*, and *mite* refer to

    a. dwellings.
    b. fish.
    c. roads.
    d. money.

31. The statement best describing the Jordan River is

    a. a gentle, level marshland.

    b. the saltiest body of water on earth.

    c. a swift-currented body of water fouled by ooze and slime
       which moves southward through scraggly vegetation
       and over poisonous soil.

    d. a straight, southward-moving, fresh-water channel which
       is usually dry except during periods of heavy rain.

32. After the infant Jesus was presented in the temple, His family immediately returned to

    a. Jerusalem.
    b. Bethlehem.
    c. Nazareth.
    d. Capernaum.

33. The Apostle Paul was a product of three cultures:

    a. Persian, Greek, and Roman.
    b. Jewish, Egyptian, and Roman.
    c. Greek, Egyptian, and Roman.
    d. Jewish, Greek, and Roman.

34. The group of plants mentioned in Matthew's gospel are

    a. lilies, mint, and mustard seeds.
    b. cucumbers, melons, garlic, leeks, and onions.
    c. gopher wood, lentils, and mandrakes.
    d. bulrushes, coriander, and cinnamon.

35. The natural disaster leading to the conversion of a Philippian jailer was

    a. a typhoon.
    b. a hailstorm.
    c. an earthquake.
    d. severe lightning.

36. The valley lying between Jerusalem and the Mount of Olives is the

    a. Kidron Valley.
    b. Valley of Jezreel.
    c. Jordan Valley.
    d. Valley of Ajalon (Aijalon).

37. In the New Testament the Samaritans' ancestry was

    a. exclusively Jewish.
    b. part Jewish, part Gentile.
    c. Gentile.

d. unknown.

38. The country that does not border modern Israel is

    a. Jordan.
    b. Egypt.
    c. North Yemen.
    d. Lebanon.

39. The modern Jewish calendar is based on

    a. cycles of rain.
    b. planetary alignments.
    c. cycles of the moon and the seasons.
    d. the seasons.

40. Below is a map of the Mediterranean. Asia is the section of
    the map labeled

    a.   b.   c.   d.

Locations of the New Testament

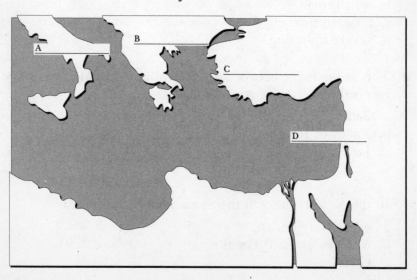

41. Greece is the section of the map labeled

    a.   b.   c.   d.

42. On his way to Rome, Paul traveled mainly

    a. on foot.
    b. by ship.
    c. on horseback.
    d. by chariot.

43. The substance not used as a spice or perfume was

    a. spikenard (nard).
    b. aloe.
    c. barley.
    d. myrrh.

44. Jesus' early ministry, the Sermon on the Mount, and the healing of the centurion's servant occurred in

    a. the province of Galilee.
    b. the province of Samaria.
    c. the province of Judea.
    d. the province of Perea.

45. If you were on the road going from Jerusalem to Jericho, a road often taken by Jesus, you would generally be walking

    a. west, northwest, on level ground.
    b. east, northeast, downhill.
    c. east, northeast, uphill.
    d. directly north, skirting the Dead Sea.

46. In Jesus' day, Israel was called

    a. Palestine.
    b. Canaan.
    c. Jordan.
    d. The United Arab Emirates.

47. The city associated with Bartimaeus and Zacchaeus is

    a. Damascus.

b. Jerusalem.
c. Nazareth.
d. Jericho.

48. The approximate distance from Bethlehem to Jerusalem is

   a. one mile.
   b. five miles.
   c. twenty-five miles.
   d. seventy miles.

49. An occupational group despised by the Jews in Jesus' day was

   a. beggars.
   b. tax collectors.
   c. lawyers (scribes).
   d. fishermen.

50. The city where the disciples of Jesus were first called "Christians" and where Paul began his missionary journeys was

   a. Jerusalem.
   b. Antioch.
   c. Ephesus.
   d. Damascus.

Answers

1. (d.) Egypt, a desert plateau, occupied the northeast corner of Africa. The heart of the country was a 600-mile valley, stretching from Aswan in the south to the Mediterranean Sea in the north, through which the Nile River ran. Egypt offered sanctuary to some of God's choicest people. Famine brought Abraham, who hobnobbed with royalty and departed even wealthier than when he arrived. Famine also brought Jacob who enjoyed a secure retirement there. Centuries later, when God sent His Son into the world, Egypt, which swaddled the infant nation of Israel in the days of Moses, draped its protec-

tion over the nation's infant Redeemer in the days of Herod. Egypt is mentioned in thirty-three books of the Bible.

2. (b.) Assyria, which enjoyed world power during the 9–7th centuries B.C., was the northern neighbor of Babylonia in Mesopotamia. In 721 Assyria captured Samaria, the capital of the northern kingdom of Israel. Assyria deported thousands of Jews to Nineveh, the Assyrian capital, and to other places of servitude. Nineveh, located on the Tigris River, was one of the world's oldest "large" cities. King Sennacherib adorned Nineveh with grand building projects, financed with the tribute of vassal rulers like Hezekiah of Judah (2 Kings 18:14). Nineveh was a wicked city, known for its fertility cult worship and the gruesome treatment it imposed on conquered nations.

3. (c.) The Persian Empire spread from India to Egypt. After capturing Babylon in 538 B.C., Cyrus, king of Persia, allowed the Jews to return to Jerusalem. A large portion of Scripture describes the Jews' "Persian period." Esther, Ezra, Nehemiah, Isaiah, Daniel, Haggai, Zechariah, and Malachi wrote about Persia's dominance.

4. (d.) Although Scripture states that Isaac "sowed in that land [Philistia], and reaped in the same year a hundredfold" (Genesis 26:12), the patriarchs were primarily herdsmen, nomad-sojourners who tended their flocks. Jacob's skill as a stockman was legendary. His system of breeding livestock by striped rods and water troughs seems bizarre, but his "insider information" made him an exceedingly prosperous cattleman.

5. (d.) A number of significant things happened to Moses at Mount Sinai, which is also called Horeb and "the mountain of God." There Moses received his "burning bush commission," the Ten Commandments, the law, and the blueprints for the tabernacle.

6. (c.) Under Levitical law unclean animals, such as pigs, camels, and rabbits, were not to be eaten. Biblical references to pigs were unfavorable. Yet domestic and wild pigs abounded in Bible times. The New Testament notes two pig farms: one where the prodigal son came to his senses (Luke 15), and the other at Gadara, where Jesus cast the demons into the swine (Matthew 8:28–34).

7. (a.) Israel, a very small (longitudinally narrow) country, has only one time zone. From the Mediterranean to the Sea of Galilee, the country is only thirty miles wide. From the Mediterranean to the southern end of the Dead Sea, the distance is around eighty-five miles.

8. (d.) When King David captured the Jebusite fortress on Mount Zion, "Zion" and "the city of David" became synonymous with Jerusalem. Gradually, the Temple Mount, north of Zion, and its surrounding areas were absorbed by the city. Jerusalem at an elevation of 2,439 feet is one of the world's highest capitals.

9. (a.) The Negev refers only to the dry region in the far south of Israel that merges with the Sinai peninsula. Beersheba, the city where Abraham and Isaac dug wells, is in the Negev.

10. (c.) Jerusalem, along with Bethlehem, Hebron, Bethel, Samaria, Shechem, Nazareth, and Megiddo, are all located in the Western Plateau or "hill country" of Israel.

11. (b.) In Canaan, life depended on water. People and cattle gathered daily at wells. Therefore, it is not surprising that relationships began there.

12. (c.) Climate includes four factors: terrain (altitude, the lay of the land, etc.); the relationship of the land to other landforms or bodies of water; air currents; and latitude. With two, well-defined seasons (hot/dry in summer, warm/wet in winter), Israel lies at a latitude of 29–33 degrees north and experiences both sea breezes and desert winds. The climate closely parallels that of Palm Springs, California.

13. (b.) Although its exact location is not known, Eden was a peaceful, productive garden in Mesopotamia's Fertile Crescent between the Tigris and the Euphrates rivers. As the only human inhabitants of Eden, Adam and Eve enjoyed unprecedented relationships with their Creator, their environment, and with each other.

14. (c.) The north-south distance from Dan to Beersheba is just under 150 miles, roughly the distance between the following pairs of cities: Orlando and Jacksonville, Florida; Dallas and Wichita Falls, Texas; and Cleveland and Columbus, Ohio.

15. (c.) The Mediterranean, also called the Great Sea, forms the western border of Israel and greatly affects its climate.

16. (d.) The Nile originates in equatorial Africa in the waters of Lakes Victoria, Albert, and Edward. From Lake Victoria to the Mediterranean is 2,450 air miles. The Nile's circuitous route of 4,150 miles makes it the longest river in the world. Over the years the Nile has irrigated farms and deposited a thick layer of precious silt in the Nile Valley. When God plagued Pharaoh, the life-giving Nile turned to blood.

17. (a.) The Euphrates, one of Eden's four rivers, flowed from modern day Turkey through Mesopotamia and joined the Tigris River just north of the Persian Gulf. Crossing the Euphrates often served as a Biblical milestone. Abraham crossed the Euphrates on his way to Canaan. Jacob crossed when he fled Laban. Crossing the river caused the exiled Israelites to weep for Jerusalem. Before Armageddon, the Euphrates will dry up to allow the kings from the East to advance on Israel.

18. (c.) Gilgal was the encampment near the Jordan through which the Israelites entered the Promised Land and from which they attacked nearby Jericho.

19. (a.) Noah's ark came to rest on Ararat in Turkey or Armenia 150 days after the rains began (Genesis 8).

20. (b.) The land of Goshen in Egypt's fertile delta was prime real estate for cattlemen. Pharaoh considered it "the best of the land" (Genesis 47:6) and grazed his own herds there.

21. (a.) The Western Plateau of Israel contained many caves. The cave at Mamre near Hebron was called Machpelah. The burial plot was the only land Abraham ever owned in Canaan.

22. (d.) After David was crowned king over all Israel, he captured Jerusalem and made it the nation's capital. During the reigns of David and Solomon, the city enjoyed prosperity. Between 925 B.C. and 586 B.C. the city declined. Jerusalem was plundered or besieged by the Egyptians, the Philistines, the Arabians, and the Syrians. Jerusalem was destroyed by Nebuchadnezzar around 586 B.C. Reconstruction of Jerusalem began after the decree of Cyrus around 536 B.C. At the time of Christ, the Romans had been entrenched in the city for about fifty years.

23. (c.) Jacob promised that a lion of the tribe of Judah would one day rule Israel (Genesis 49:9–10). Samson killed a

lion, and his boastful riddle about the feat led to judgment on the Philistines (Judges 14–15). Daniel's night in the lion's den proved to King Darius that the God of Daniel "is the living God." (Daniel 6).

24. (d.) King Solomon was not frequently attacked by anyone. The name *Solomon* means "peaceable." According to the King, there was "neither adversary nor misfortune" (1 Kings 5:4) in Israel. Those tranquil conditions allowed him to build the Temple and his own palace (1 Kings 6–7).

25. (c.) Babylon stood on a broad plain in Mesopotamia. The city was fifteen miles square and was protected by high, broad walls on which chariot races were run. Babylon spanned the Euphrates and showcased the Hanging Gardens. Ishtar Gate, one of Nebuchadnezzar's famed building projects, was a forty-foot high entrance adorned with 575 enameled dragons, bulls, and lions. The gate opened into Procession Street, Babylon's equivalent to Pennsylvania Avenue in Washington, D.C. The palace boasted a banquet hall 56 feet wide and 168 feet long. Ordinary houses were three or four stories high, and streets, named for gods, ran in straight lines.

Babylon was a religious center, housing nearly 600 temples, altars, and shrines. Its economy was service oriented and the Jews became involved with insurance, real estate, and international banking. The synagogue evolved as the Jewish worship center in Babylon.

26. (b.) Two chapters in the Bible deal with Creation, but fifty chapters mention the tabernacle in the wilderness. The tabernacle was a tent which contained two rooms—the Holy Place and the Holy of Holies. The Holy Place contained tools for worship: the table of shewbread, the golden candlestick, and the altar of incense. The ark of the covenant was in the Holy of Holies. A rectangular, curtain-enclosed court surrounded the tabernacle.

27. (a.) The plagues involved: the water of the Nile (Exodus 7: 14–25), frogs (8:6–15), lice or gnats (8:16–19), flies (8:20–32), livestock (9:1–7), boils (9:8–12), hail (9:13–35), locusts (10:1–20), darkness (10:21–29), and the death of the firstborn (11–12:30). God did plague Israel with quail enroute to the Promised Land

ᵓers 11:31–32), but this calamity occurred long after the plagᵘ ᵉs in Egypt.

28. (d.) The Dead Sea, also called the Salt Sea, measures fifty-three miles in length and ten miles in width. At 1300 feet below sea level, it is the lowest point on earth. (California's Death Valley is only 282 feet below sea level.) The Dead Sea has no outlet for the water it receives except evaporation. At 26–35 percent salinity, it is the saltiest body of water on earth. By comparison, Utah's Great Salt Lake is only 18 percent saline.

29. (b.) The Jordan, Israel's chief river, carries water from the Sea of Galilee to the Dead Sea. The river is entirely below sea level (see answer 31).

30. (d.) New Testament Jews dealt with the coins of three nations. The denarius was a Roman coin. The drachma was Greek. The only coin the Jews minted was the mite which the widow put into the treasury (Mark 12:42). Coins were made of bronze, copper, gold, or silver. Coinage was based on ancient weights such as the shekel or mina. Since the values of these weights differed from country to country, moneychangers were a necessary part of society.

31. (c.) Although 65 air miles separate the Sea of Galilee from the Dead Sea, the Jordan River meanders for 200 miles over nitrous soil and scrubby thickets. Between the Sea of Galilee and the Dead Sea the Jordan drops in elevation at the rate of nearly forty feet per mile, causing a strong current. In many areas, adjacent mudbanks foul the water. The Jordan is not navigable and boasts no sizable city along its banks. It is not surprising that Naaman the leper preferred the rivers of Damascus to the Jordan.

32. (c.) Forty days after His birth, Jesus was presented in the temple in Jerusalem. Luke wrote: "And when they had performed everything according to the law of the Lord, they returned to Galilee, to their own city of Nazareth" (Luke 2:39).

33. (d.) The Jews gave Paul his pedigree, as evidenced by his name, Saul; his career choice of Pharisee; and his association with Rabbi Gamaliel. The Greeks influenced Paul's intellect. His pastoral letters are classics in the Greek language, and his knowledge of *koine* Greek enabled him to preach without lan-

guage barriers. The Romans bestowed citizenship and privilege. Paul traveled at will, invoked legal protection as necessary, and moved with ease among Roman aristocracy.

34. (a.) Matthew reminded his readers to observe the lilies of the field, to tithe more important things than mint, and to view faith and the kingdom of heaven in terms of a mustard seed.

35. (c.) While the earthquake at Philippi was the only one recorded on the missionary journeys, Paul was accustomed to tremors. The Jordan Valley, part of the Afro-Arabian Rift Valley, is one of the longest, deepest, and widest fissures in the earth's surface. Between 200–300 earthquakes are recorded daily in Israel. The earth shook at Sinai when the law was given (Exodus 19:18), when Jesus died (Matthew 27:54), and when He rose (Matthew 28:2). A great earthquake will occur during the Tribulation (Revelation 16:16-21).

36. (a.) The Kidron Valley separates the eastern section of Jerusalem from the Mount of Olives. When Absalom usurped the throne, David under political duress fled Jerusalem across the Kidron Valley. Ten centuries later, Jesus left Jerusalem under spiritual duress, crossed the Kidron, and sought refuge at Gethsemane.

37. (b.) The Samaritans were full-blooded Jews until the Assyrians captured the northern kingdom of Israel in 722 B.C. Many Jews were deported to Assyrian cities, but some remained in Samaria and intermarried with the Assyrian colonists who re-settled the area. Jews in the southern kingdom were outraged by the marriages and by the Samaritan practice of combining pagan rituals with the worship of Jehovah (syncretism). The Samaritans honored the Pentateuch but only in the Samaritan language. They believed Samaria was the nation chosen to point mankind to salvation. They expected Messiah but not from the Davidic line. Their concept of worship was place (Mount Gerizim) and ritual, without regard to the nature of God.

38. (c.) Israel is bounded by Lebanon on the north, Syria and Jordan on the east, and Egypt on the south. North Yemen is along the southern border of Saudi Arabia.

39. (c.) The modern Jewish calendar is soli-lunar, which means it is based on both the lunar cycles and the four seasons which are determined by the sun. Each month of the Jewish calendar begins with a new moon. Since a solar year of 365 days is longer than twelve lunar months, an extra month is added periodically to correct the difference. The Jewish calendar stands in contrast to our Gregorian calendar which is purely solar. The modern Jewish calendar begins on Rosh Hashanah during September or October.

40. (c.) Asia, whenever mentioned in the New Testament, refers to the Roman province that occupied the western third of Turkey, not to the continent of Asia. Although Pergamum was the official capital, Ephesus was "the first and the greatest metropolis of Asia." Paul spent more time in Ephesus than any other city. He undoubtedly saw the temple of Artemis, enjoyed the magnificent harbor, and walked in the well-stocked marketplace. Ephesus was a crossroads for both shipping and land travel. Many Christians left Ephesus for Rome — to be fed to the lions — so many, in fact, that Ignatius called Ephesus "the highway of martyrs." The book of Revelation is addressed to the seven churches in Asia: Ephesus, Smyrna, Pergamum, Thyatira, Sardis, Philadelphia, and Laodicea.

41. (b.) Bounded on the east by the Aegean and on the west by the Ionian Sea, Greece, a peninsula nation in the Mediterranean, was the focus of Paul's second missionary journey. Paul wrote five letters to the Greek Christians: 1 and 2 Thessalonians, 1 and 2 Corinthians, and Philippians.

42. (b.) Paul's voyage to Rome is recorded in Acts 27–28. Tourists, businessmen, soldiers, and government officials crossed the Mediterranean. While sea travel was popular, it was not easy. Winds sidetracked Paul's ship near Crete. At Malta, he and 276 other passengers swam for their lives.

43. (c.) Next to wheat, barley was the most important grain in Israel. Barley had a short growing season and could be cultivated in both poor and fertile soils. Barley, the "poor man's grain," sustained Ruth and Naomi (Ruth 3:17). Five barley loaves fed five thousand at Galilee.

44. (a.) Galilee was a Roman province in northern Israel. The area was geographically divided into Upper Galilee, a

sparsely populated, mountainous plateau, and Lower Galilee, a combination of highlands and valleys. Lower Galilee was on the east–west trade routes through the Valley of Jezreel. Many travelers lingered in Lower Galilee, for the area was known as "Galilee of the Nations." Much of Jesus' ministry centered in Lower Galilee: Cana, Capernaum, Chorazin, Nain, Nazareth, and the Sea of Galilee.

45. (b.) The road from Jerusalem to Jericho was downhill. Jericho, lodged in the Jordan Valley and situated fourteen miles east-northeast of Jerusalem, is 820 feet *below sea level*. Jerusalem, nestled in the "hills" of the western plateau, is 2,439 feet *above sea level*. A traveler going from Jericho to Jerusalem would actually climb 3,259 feet before entering (probably exhausted) the gates of Jerusalem. A pregnant Mary made this journey to register for taxes.

46. (a.) Israel's New Testament name, Palestine, means "the land of the Philistines." The title was given by the Greeks who invaded the coast and remembered its ancient inhabitants.

47. (d.) There have been three Jerichos. The first Jericho, home to Rahab the harlot, was destroyed when the Israelites invaded the Promised Land. The second Jericho, built on a slightly different site, was the winter capital of Herod and was familiar to Jesus, Bartimaeus, and Zacchaeus. The third Jericho is the modern city, built on a slightly different site from its namesakes.

48. (b.) Bethlehem, a holding place for the sheep used in the temple, was a little over five miles from Jerusalem. Christmas card artists embellish the little town with shepherds and wise men. There is no doubt that there were plenty of shepherds in the fields to celebrate Jesus' birth. But the wise men, unless they arrived within the Baby's first forty days never went to Bethlehem (see answer 32). About the only thing of geographical significance in the town was the well. King David offered a cup of Bethlehem's cool, sweet water in worship to God.

49. (b.) Taxes may plague Americans, but our assessments are light compared to the Jews. Not only did the Jew pay taxes to maintain Jewish society, he was also a heavy contributor to the Roman Empire. The Romans franchised local Jews to collect the taxes for a district. This tax collector, known as a publi-

can, often leased part of his territory to a junior collector who not only gathered tribute for Rome but also for his benefactor and himself as well. Publicans, such as Matthew Levi, financially bled their own people for the glory of Rome and for personal profit.

50. (b.) Antioch gained Biblical significance in the book of Acts. After persecution broke out in Jerusalem, several believers moved north to Syria and formed the church at Antioch, which later supported Paul's missionary journeys. At Antioch the disciples were first called Christians. The city was one of the few places in the New Testament where the preaching of the gospel did not incite riots.

TWO

ABOUT THE BIBLE

"AND NOW WE COME TO THE FRENCH . . ."

Amid sighs and glances at wristwatches, the tour climbed the last set of stairs and obediently trudged behind their guide. Fatigue and cultural overkill had taken their toll.

"I apologize for the incovenience. We are having trouble with our elevators and the air conditioning seems a bit off up here."

The sweaty group nodded agreement.

"This is our last stop," the guide went on.

A few faces perked up, glancing about the exhibition room, well-stocked with furniture.

A lady looked at a curious chair. "It looks too uncomfortable to even want to sit on," she murmured to a companion.

"Madame, that's a Louis XIII, " the guide cued off the comment.

"Oh, a Louis!" she said at first, startled by the attention. Then, frustration took over. "Frankly, that doesn't mean a thing to me. It looks like a skinny chair. I don't know one Louis from the other, and I don't know how the French keep them straight."

"It's simple, Madame. It's a matter of organization. Start with the popular kings—Louis XIII-XVI. The period and furniture of Louis XIII is called Louis Treize. Louis XIV is Louis Quatorze. Louis XV is Louis Quinze, and Louis XVI is Louis Seize."

Madame cocked her head, a little bewildered.

29

"Now every king had a mate, a minister, and a motto that somehow affected him. If you know something about the man, it's easy to recognize his chair."

"Oh, really?"

"Louis XIII was too busy watching over things to ever have a really comfortable chair. He couldn't relax for a minute. That's why this piece suits him."

The guide pushed the shallow-seated, angular, low-backed chair to the center of the platform.

"Louis XIII struggled to assert himself, first with his mother, then with the wife his mother chose, and finally with his minister, Richelieu. Louis XIII often repeated his motto, 'Now I am king,' mostly to remind himself just who was king. There could be no soft, plump chair for this man. He had to be alert."

"Whose chair is that?"

"That belonged to the extravagant Louis XIV. Notice the back. It's tall because the king was short. Louis XIV liked the illusion of height. He always tried to appear taller. He wore high heels and bouffant wigs and married the small Marie Thérèse of Spain. The king was rather . . . , well, plain. He surrounded himself with ornate things. His clever and resourceful finance minster, Colbert, worked hard to keep the king looking tall and adorned with finery, but Louis outlived and outspent him."

Slowly, the guide painted small pictures of the monarchs and their furniture. Against the backdrop of mates and ministers and mottos, the kingly personalities took shape and the weary audience perked up.

For many of us, our first dozen encounters with the Bible are similar to a trip through French period furniture: it doesn't mean anything! The Bible is a fat book full of words. We don't know a Levite from a Hittite, and we're not sure anyone else does.

Once we discover there is organization to the Bible and grasp a few key ideas, we find ourselves drawn in. We befriend personalities, like Moses or Paul. We stumble across a few famous quotes. Our vocabularies expand. We read more. We may not understand everything, but we know we understand something.

As we read, think about, and apply Scripture, we slowly glean (a descriptive term for the process) principles and concepts from God's Word. Like spiritual bricklayers, we construct bulwarks—load-bearing walls upon which we build our faith.

"About the Bible" tests the strength of our scriptural bulwarks. For new Bible readers, the questions introduce concepts. For seasoned readers, the questions provide scope.

Questions

1. The Protestant Bible contains
    a. twenty-seven books.
    b. thirty-nine books.
    c. sixty-six books.
    d. seventy-five books.

2. The word *gospel* means
    a. "the refuge."
    b. "good news."
    c. "betrothal."
    d. "an agreement."

For questions 3–6, identify the book which begins or ends with the quoted, well-known verses:

3. "In the beginning God created the heavens and the earth."
    a. Genesis
    b. John
    c. Hebrews
    d. Revelation

4. "In those days there was no king in Israel; everyone did what was right in his own eyes."
    a. Genesis
    b. 1 Samuel
    c. Judges

d. 1 Kings

5. "Go therefore and make disciples of all the nations, baptizing them in the name of the Father and the Son and the Holy Spirit, teaching them to observe all that I commanded you; and lo, I am with you always, even to the end of the age."
    a. Matthew
    b. Mark
    c. Luke
    d. John

6. "In the beginning was the Word, and the Word was with God, and the Word was God."
    a. Genesis
    b. John
    c. Hebrews
    d. Revelation

7. The foundational teaching on justification, sanctification, and glorification is found in
    a. Leviticus 23.
    b. 1 Corinthians 12, 13, and 15.
    c. James 3.
    d. Romans 6–8.

8. In the citation in Luke 2:1–3, the number 2 refers to
    a. the testament.
    b. the chapter.
    c. the verse.
    d. the paragraph.

9. "Blessed are the poor in spirit, for theirs is the kingdom of God" is an example of
    a. the Ten Commandments.
    b. fruits of the Spirit.
    c. the Beatitudes.
    d. the Lord's Prayer.

10. The word *amen* means

    a. "our Lord, come."
    b. "so be it."
    c. "praise God."
    d. all of the above.

11. Manna was

    a. a shibboleth.
    b. Mammon.
    c. God's glory.
    d. food.

12. The Protestant Old Testament contains

    a. twenty-four books.
    b. twenty-seven books.
    c. thirty-nine books.
    d. forty-eight books.

13. This well-known passage, "For God so loved the world, that He gave His only begotten Son, that whoever believes in Him should not perish but have everlasting life," is followed by the verse,

    a. "For God did not send the Son into the world to judge the world, but that the world should be saved through Him."

    b. "Truly, truly, I say to you, unless one is born again, he cannot see the kingdom of God."

    c. "Simon Peter answered Him, 'Lord, to whom shall we go? You have words of eternal life.'"

    d. "And behold, one came to Him and said, 'Teacher, what good thing shall I do that I may obtain eternal life?'"

14. Genesis is called the

    a. Book of Beginnings.
    b. Apocalypse.
    c. Song of Songs.

d. Book of Comfort.

15. The classic definition of faith is

   a. "He who was revealed in the flesh, was vindicated in the Spirit, beheld by angels, proclaimed among the nations, believed on in the world, taken up in glory."

   b. "not that we loved God, but that He loved us and sent His Son to be the propitiation for our sins."

   c. "the fruit of lips that give thanks to His name."

   d. "the assurance of things hoped for, the conviction of things not seen."

16. The Ten Commandments are found in

   a. Genesis 3.
   b. Exodus 3.
   c. Genesis 12.
   d. Exodus 20.

17. The statement, ". . . no prophecy of Scripture is a matter of one's own interpretation, for no prophecy was ever made by an act of human will, but men moved by the Holy Spirit spoke from God," was made by

   a. Isaiah.
   b. Peter.
   c. Jesus.
   d. Moses.

18. The first five books of the Old Testament were written by

   a. Abraham.
   b. Moses.
   c. Joshua.
   d. David.

19. The symbol associated with Christ is

   a. the Alpha and the Omega.
   b. the valley of dry bones.

c. a roaring lion.

d. candlesticks.

20. The Great Tribulation is the name of

    a. the Assyrian Captivity.
    b. the Babylonian Captivity.
    c. a future period of great calamity on earth.
    d. the Jewish rebellion against Rome in A.D. 68–70.

21. Abib, Tishri, and Adar were

    a. cities in Babylon.
    b. Solomon's chief wives.
    c. three Hebrews in the fiery furnace.
    d. months in the Jewish calendar.

22. The ark of the covenant was

    a. another name for the Tabernacle.
    b. a sacred, rectangular box covered by the mercy seat.
    c. Noah's ark.
    d. the high priest's breastplate.

23. The three phrases, "the blind leading the blind," "a generation of vipers," and "whitewashed tombs," all refer to

    a. Pharisees.
    b. leaders of Rome.
    c. tax collectors.
    d. the unbelieving masses.

24. Nathan's story of the rich man who stole the poor man's lamb was a metaphor for the actual event of

    a. Gehazi's greed.
    b. two mothers, a healthy infant, and a dead infant.
    c. Johnathan's defense of David.
    d. David's sin with Bathsheba.

25. The phrase "a Triune God" means

    a. God is all-knowing.

b. God is one God and yet three Persons.
c. God reveals Himself through His names.
d. God is absolute.

26. The first five books of the Old Testament are called

a. the Law.
b. the Torah.
c. the Pentateuch.
d. all of the above.

27. Some Bible names are associated with unique character traits. Select the *incorrect* match:

a. Methuselah — a very old person
b. Judas — betrayer
c. Jonah — patience
d. Ananias — liar

28. Diana, Dagon, Molech, Ashtaroth, and Baal were

a. judges of Israel.
b. pagan gods and goddesses.
c. Egyptian rulers.
d. Gentile rulers of Israel.

29. The Old Testament verse that is most frequently quoted in the New Testament is

> The Lord says to my Lord:
> "Sit at My right hand,
> Until I make Thine enemies a
>   footstool for Thy feet."

It is found in the Old Testament book of

a. Proverbs.
b. Job.
c. Psalms.
d. Deuteronomy.

30. The major divisions of the Old Testament are

    a. historical, poetical, and prophetical books.
    b. historical books, prophetical books, and epistles.
    c. historical books and prophetical books.
    d. historical and poetical books.

31. Associated with testing and trials is the number

    a. seven.
    b. twelve.
    c. forty.
    d. seventy.

32. The verse that is a doxology is

    a. "But as for you, speak the things which are fitting for sound doctrine."

    b. "Now to the King eternal, immortal, invisible, the only God, be honor and glory forever and ever. Amen."

    c. "But the fruit of the Spirit is love, joy, peace, patience, kindness, goodness, faithfulness."

    d. "Greet Prisca and Aquila, and the household of Onesiphorus."

33. The only Gentile to write a New Testament book was

    a. Matthew.
    b. Peter.
    c. Luke.
    d. Paul.

34. An allegory is

    a. a special inheritance given to the oldest son.
    b. a sacrifice.
    c. a genealogy.
    d. a story where fictional characters and actions represent a greater truth.

35. The "good news" (gospel) is that

    a. God has the power to save all who believe in Jesus Christ.
    b. the wages of sin is death.
    c. salvation comes through church membership.
    d. all men are God's children.

36. The fate of a scapegoat was that

    a. it was slain.
    b. it was kept as a pet.
    c. it was sold.
    d. it was driven into the wilderness.

37. A tithe is

    a. a farm tool.
    b. a parcel of land.
    c. a tenth of one's income.
    d. a bundle of grain stalks.

38. The term *holy* means

    a. "set apart, chosen."
    b. "promised."
    c. "prosperous, wealthy."
    d. "sorrowful."

39. The occasion described beginning with the verses, "Now it came about in those days that a decree went out from Caesar Augustus, that a census be taken of all the inhabited earth," refers to

    a. The marriage feast of Cana.
    b. Jesus' birth.
    c. Pentecost.
    d. the Sermon on the Mount.

40. *Apostasy* means

    a. inwardly rejecting God's truth while outwardly maintaining some form of religious practice.

b. strict adherence to God's Word.
c. government based on God's principles.
d. rule by Gentile nations.

41. The word *testament* means

a. "custom or habit."
b. "story."
c. "covenant or agreement."
d. "commandment."

42. The millennium will be characterized by

a. natural disasters.
b. wars.
c. satanic rule.
d. justice.

43. The synoptic Gospels are

a. Matthew, Mark, and Luke.
b. Mark and John.
c. Matthew, Luke, and John.
d. Matthew and John.

44. "The Lord bless you, and keep you; the Lord make His face shine on you, and be gracious to you; the Lord lift up His countenance on you, and give you peace." This verse is known as

a. a vow.
b. a doxology.
c. intercessory prayer.
d. a benediction.

45. Jesus was presented as a "suffering servant" in the gospel written by

a. Matthew.
b. Mark.
c. Luke.
d. John.

46. The word *Bible* means

    a. "book."
    b. "story."
    c. "salvation."
    d. "good news."

47. Identify the following verse that is messianic in theme.

    a. "So the wall was completed. . . . And it came about when all our enemies heard of it, and all the nations surrounding us saw it, they lost their confidence; for they recognized that this work had been accomplished with the help of our God."

    b. "And who knows whether you have not attained royalty for such a time as this?"

    c. "Rejoice greatly, O daughter of Zion! Shout in triumph, O daughter of Jerusalem! Behold, your king is coming to you; He is just and endowed with salvation, humble, and mounted on a donkey, even on a colt, the foal of a donkey."

    d. "I call heaven and earth to witness against you today, that I have set before you life and death, the blessing and the curse."

48. God's *full armor*—the "breastplate of righteousness," the "shield of faith," the "helmet of Salvation," and prayer—was to be used against

    a. Sennacherib.
    b. the devil.
    c. Goliath.
    d. Nebuchadnezzar.

49. Blasphemy is

    a. showing contempt for God.
    b. having great trouble or pain.
    c. setting something or someone aside for service to God.
    d. looting after a battle.

50. The event that commemorates Christ's death, seals the New Covenant, and demonstrates the unity and faith of the church body is

    a. the Last Supper.
    b. Pentecost.
    c. the Lord's Supper.
    d. the Lord's Day.

Answers

1. (c.) The Protestant Bible contains sixty-six books. The Roman Catholic Bible adds a set of books called the Apocrypha. The Eastern Orthodox Bible adds a similar set but refers to it as the Deuterocanonicals ("secondary rule"). The Hebrew Bible consists of the Old Testament alone.

2. (b.) *Gospel* means "good news." We think of *gospel* as a New Testament word, but the term was used commonly in King David's day. Isaiah tied the word *gospel* to Israel's coming Messiah 650 years before Christ's birth (Isaiah 40:9; 41:27; 52:7; 61:1). When Mark 1:1 began, "The beginning of the gospel," the use of this well-known word was significant!

3. (a.) Genesis 1:1

4. (c.) Judges 21:25 (see also 17:6, 18:1, and 19:1).

5. (a.) Matthew 28:19–20

6. (b.) John 1:1

7. (d.) Romans 6–8 contains the foundational teaching on justification, sanctification, and glorification.

8. (b.) The number *2* in Luke 2:1–3 indicates the chapter.

9. (c.) The beatitudes are found in Matthew 5.

10. (b.) *Amen* means "so be it." Although the word usually concludes a prayer, Jesus occasionally used the word *amen* to emphasize the reality of what He was about to say: "Truly, truly, I say to you, the Son can do nothing of Himself, unless it is something He sees the Father doing." (John 5:19). Some translations use the words *verily, verily,* but all stem from the word *amen.*

11. (d.) Manna was "bread from heaven" or "bread of angels" (Psalm 78:25). The food resembled fine, flake-like seed, was white in color, and tasted like wafers mixed with honey

(Exodus 16:4, 14, 31). Manna was provided until the Israelites crossed into the Promised Land. Revelation 2:17 promises "hidden manna" to the one who overcomes.

12. (c.) There are thirty-nine books in the Protestant Old Testament.

13. (a.) John 3:17 unmistakably identifies Jesus Christ as the focus of salvation.

14. (a.) Genesis is called "the Book of Beginnings," an appropriate title, since Genesis introduces the major themes of the Bible.

15. (d.) According to Hebrews 11:1, "faith is the assurance of things hoped for, the conviction of things not seen."

16. (d.) The first listing of the Ten Commandments is Exodus 20.

17. (b.) The quote is from 2 Peter 1:20–21. Peter, the uneducated fisherman, well understood that it was the Holy Spirit who enabled him to pen the words of Scripture and debate the religious leaders of Jerusalem.

18. (b.) Moses is credited with the authorship of the first five books of the Old Testament. Although Moses never identified himself as the author, prophets like Daniel (9:11–13) and Malachi (4:4), and Jesus (Matthew 8:4), attested to the fact.

19. (a.) The Alpha and the Omega are the first and last letters of the Greek alphabet and symbolize Christ's eternal nature (Revelation 1:8,11; 21:6; 22:13).

20. (c.) Although "tribulation" refers to any affliction or suffering, Daniel 12:1, Jeremiah 30:7, and Matthew 24:21 predict a specific period of calamity and judgment. Scholars differ as to when the Great Tribulation will occur in the prophetic scenario, but it is generally considered a future event.

21. (d.) Passover and the Feast of Unleavened Bread occurred during the month *Abib* (March/April). The Feast of Trumpets, the Day of Atonement, and the Festival of Tabernacles came during *Tishri* (September/October). Purim was celebrated during *Adar* (February/March).

22. (b.) The ark of the covenant, or the "ark of God," was a wooden box overlaid with gold. It was roughly four and one-half feet long, two and one-half feet wide, and two and one-half feet high. The box was covered by a lid adorned with the fig-

ures of two cherubim. The ark contained the Ten Commandments, manna, and Aaron's rod. The ark was a significant, visible sign that God identified Himself with Israel.

23. (a.) Jesus' most scathing remarks are directed to the Pharisees. Consider Matthew 15:14; 23:33 and Luke 11:40; 12:1.

24. (d.) Nathan's story has little impact without an understanding of its context. The story exposed the adultery of David with Bathsheba (2 Samuel 12:1–15).

25. (b.) Triune relates to the Trinity, a spiritual reality which defies human understanding. Daniel Webster was once asked, "How can you reconcile the doctrine of the Trinity with reason?" The statesman replied, "Do you expect to understand the arithmetic of Heaven?" The arithmetic of the Trinity asserts that there is one God with three personal, unified identities. Although the word *Trinity* does not explicitly occur in the Bible, the trinitarian concept is found in the Hebrew name *Elohim*, the plural noun used for God in Genesis 1:1. In the New Testament, the existence of and interplay among the three Persons of the Trinity are mentioned in Matthew 28:19; Luke 1:35–37; John 14:26; 15:26; 2 Corinthians 13:14; and 1 Peter 1:2.

26. (d.) The Jews called the first five books of the Old Testament, the Law. In the Hebrew, the books were known as the Torah; in the Greek, the Pentateuch.

27. (c.) Jonah was a jinx! When the prophet boarded the ship bound for Tarshish, he publicized the fact that he was fleeing from God. Whether his shipmates believed him in port, we don't know. But in the midst of a tempest, they gave Jonah's story a second thought. Eventually, the sailors threw Jonah overboard where he was swallowed by a fish. Even though the sailors came to fear the Lord and Jonah went on to deliver the Ninevehites from judgment, a "Jonah" means a person who brings ill-fortune.

28. (b.) Pagan religions centered around this dubious quintet. Diana, also called Artemis, was a goddess of the Ephesians (Acts 19:24–28), while Ashtaroth was a Canaanite goddess (Judges 2:11–13). The rest were gods. Baal belonged to the Canaanites (Numbers 22:41), Dagon to the Philistines (1 Samuel

5:2–5), and Molech to the Ammonites (Leviticus 18:21; 1 Kings 11:7).

29. (c.) Psalms 110:1 is quoted eighteen times in the New Testament in various forms. See Matthew 22:44 and Hebrews 12:2 for two of the occurrences.

30. (a.) The Old Testament is divided into historical, poetical, and prophetical books. There are seventeen historical and seventeen prophetical books. There are five poetical books.

31. (c.) Forty is associated with Biblical testing and trials. It rained for forty days during the Flood (Genesis 7:4). Moses spent forty days on Mount Sinai with God (Exodus 24:18). Israel spied out the land for forty days (Numbers 13:25). Goliath taunted the Israelites for forty days (1 Samuel 17:16). Nineveh had forty days to repent (Jonah 3:4), and Jesus was tested by Satan for forty days (Mark 1:13).

32. (b.) A doxology, such as the one from 1 Timothy 1:17, is a short prayer of praise directed toward God and is frequently punctuated by an "Amen."

33. (c.) Luke, the author of the longest gospel and the book of Acts, wrote more than a quarter of the New Testament. This Gentile was a physician, a historian, and a distinguished writer. His gospel is considered to be the most literary in style and emphasizes pardon, redemption, joy, and the work of the Holy Spirit.

34. (d.) An allegory is a story where fictional characters and/or actions represent greater truth. The parables are Biblical allegories. For example, Jesus explained the truth behind the "parable of the soils." The seed represented the "word of the kingdom," the sower was God's messenger, and the soils were the responses of people who heard God's word (Matthew 13:1–9, 18–23). Since every passage of Scripture is not allegorical, the Bible student must not read into passages a meaning which is not intended.

35. (a.) The gospel is the message of salvation offered by God to all who repent and believe in Jesus. The gospel focuses on man's response to the work of Christ. The epistles give many short descriptions of the gospel. See Romans 1:16; 1 Corinthians 15:3–8; Ephesians 1:13; and 2 Timothy 1:8–10.

36. (d.) Two goats were brought to the high priest on the Day of Atonement and a cast of lots decided their fates. One goat, the Lord's lot, was sacrificed; the other, the "scapegoat," became a symbol. According to Leviticus 16, Aaron would recite the sins of the people over the scapegoat's head, and then the animal was driven into the wilderness.

37. (c.) A tithe was 10 percent of one's increase—income, crops, wine, oil, and livestock. Tithing provided income for the Levites and priests and support for the widows, orphans, and strangers (Leviticus 27:30–32; Deuteronomy 14:22–29; 26:12).

38. (a.) *Holy* means "set apart" or "chosen". God is intrinsically holy. In the New Testament, holiness was a state to which God through grace called men. In response, men altered their behavior to match their state (1 Peter 1:15). This may sound like an act of will that any ordinary person could accomplish, but without the indwelling Holy Spirit man would not think in terms of holiness.

39. (b.) With the exception of the first verse of Genesis, the opening lines of Luke 2, which describe Jesus' birth, are among the most widely recognized Bible verses in the world.

40. (a.) Apostasy is a form of hypocrisy and is described in both Testaments. The apostate inwardly rejects God's truth while outwardly maintaining some form of religious practice. Some translations of the Bible substitute "rebellion" or "backsliding" for apostasy. Apostasy, a Greek term, means to "depart from" or to "fall away from" a basic doctrine. *Apostasy* is not an error in thinking or a condition prompted by ignorance. The apostate willfully abandons doctrine and defends his actions (2 Timothy 4:3–4).

41. (c.) *Testament* means covenant or agreement and comes from a Hebrew word which refers to the cut (an incision) in the sacrifice that sealed the covenant. When God promised Abram an heir (Genesis 15), the promise was sealed by offering a heifer, a goat, a ram, a turtledove, and a pigeon; the large animals were "cut" and then sacrificed (Genesis 15:1–10).

42. (d.) The Millennium, the one-thousand-year period of Christ's reign, is characterized by swift justice (Psalm 2:8–9; Jeremiah 23:5).

43. (a.) The synoptic Gospels, written by Matthew, Mark, and Luke, are somewhat biographical in nature and record similar events in Christ's life. Ninety-three percent of the gospel of John, on the other hand, covers material not mentioned by the synoptic writers. John emphasizes Jesus' time in Jerusalem, notes the Jewish feasts, and records many private conversations. John focuses on only seven miracles which he calls "signs" and records the seven "I am" statements of Christ (John 6:35–15:1).

44. (d.) The Aaronic blessing is probably the most famous benediction in the Old Testament. In Numbers 6:22–27 the Lord empowered the priests to use His name to remind the people that God was the essence of their daily lives. While we have come to associate a benediction with good things, the benediction was not a promise. Rather, it was an assurance that whatever happened, the believer was ultimately safe in God's trust (Joshua 22:6; 2 Samuel 6:18; 2 Corinthians 13:14; Hebrews 13:20–21).

45. (b.) Each gospel writer presented a different picture of Jesus. Mark presented Him as a "suffering servant." Matthew portrayed Him as the King of Israel. Luke pictured Him as the "Son of Man," and John saw the "Son of God." These snapshots of Jesus had already been captured prophetically by Isaiah. Isaiah 9:6–7 saw Jesus the King; Isaiah 42:1–7 called Him the Servant; Isaiah 7:14–16 featured Him as the Son of Man; and Isaiah 40:3–5 heralded Him as God.

46. (a.) *Bible* means "book." The Bible is a collection of books which progressively reveal God and His plan of redemption.

47. (c.) Messiah refers to the "anointed one," the Savior, who comes through the line of David. John 1:41 directly links the term *Messiah* to Jesus Christ. Messianic verses, like the one from Zechariah 9:9 (see also Matthew 21:5), are those which describe Christ's coming, His character, or His rule.

48. (b.) Believers battle spiritual foes, not physical enemies (Ephesians 6:11–20). The full armor of God is a defense against "the schemes of the devil."

49. (a.) Blasphemy, verbally showing contempt for God, was a crime punishable by stoning (Leviticus 24:16; Acts 7:54–60). The Jews charged Jesus with blasphemy (Matthew 26:65).

50. (c.) The phrase "The Lord's Supper" does not occur in the Gospels. Paul presents the concept in 1 Corinthians 11:23–30 and carefully expounds on its significance.

THREE

HISTORY: OLD TESTAMENT

ONE DRIZZLY NIGHT IN THE FOG AND MIST off the Oregon coast two beams of light groped toward each other. As they drew closer, the captain of one ship scrawled a message for his signalman to relay: "Attention. We are on a collision course. Turn your ship 10 degrees to the south."

After a few moments, the fog yielded a reply: "Sir, course confirmed. Turn your ship 10 degrees to the north."

Startled by the response, the captain dispatched another transmission. "Sir, I am an admiral in the U.S. Navy! Turn your ship 10 degrees to the south."

A prompt reply flashed back. "Sir, I am a seaman first class. Turn your ship 10 degrees to the north."

Rankled, the admiral issued his final order. "Sir, I am a battleship! Turn your ship 10 degrees to the south."

Back came the terse reply. "Sir, I am a lighthouse."

The admiral of the U.S. Navy steered his ship 10 degrees to the north. It was a matter of perspective, and neither rank, nor power, nor size could match perspective.

Many of us, even as Christians, wander through life in a spiritual fog. We hear about God. We talk about God. We have expectations about God, but our expectations often disappoint us. We ask: "Where is God?" "Does He care?" "Why do we suffer?" We yearn for a spiritual perspective.

Often, our expectations reveal a vision of God which is not Biblical. Like the admiral, we measure life by our experiences, and when God does not frame our lives according to our expectations, we pout or panic.

Who is God? What is He really like? Is He concerned about human comfort, personal security?

God provides the answers to these questions in Scripture. His responses and commands are consistent.

God cautions: "Trust My Word."

Man responds: "But, I am a better judge of the situation."

God enjoins: "Trust My Word."

Man replies, "I'm responsible for my destiny."

God says, "Trust My Word."

Man asks: "Where is God?"

God's Word is His revelation, and, apart from His revelation, no man knows God. Without knowledge of God there is no trust. Without trust there is no relationship. Without relationship there is no spiritual growth, for humans do not naturally see life from God's perspective.

Where do we find God's perspective?

Written on the pages of the Bible, particularly in the histories of the Old Testament, are a myriad of incidents from the lives of individuals, families, and nations—people who heard God's Word and whose lives changed course. Familiarity with these interactions is essential to understanding the Old Testament, in general, and God, in particular, for verse by verse these vignettes reveal God's standards, chronicle His covenants, and test His promises. From Genesis onward, God gradually reveals His character. Slowly, the spiritual fog lifts, God's agenda unfolds, and we glimpse a view of life from God's eye. Like a beacon from a lighthouse in a foggy, foreboding night, the Old Testament histories provide an unwavering perspective of God.

The questions which follow focus on the seventeen historical books of the Old Testament. The first five books span history from Creation to the Israelite's entrance into the Promised Land. The remaining twelve books chart Israel's progress as a nation, ruled first by God (Joshua, Judges, and Ruth), later by kings (Samuel, Kings, and Chronicles), and finally by foreign powers (Ezra, Nehemiah, and Esther).

NOTE: Because it is impossible to relate Old Testament history without the prophets, those prophets with historical significance are included.

Questions

1. The patriarchs of Israel were

   a. Adam, Cain, and Seth.
   b. Abraham, Isaac, and Jacob.
   c. Haran, Nahor, and Abraham.
   d. All of the above.

2. Joshua's strategy for the conquest of Canaan was to

   a. make treaties with its kings.
   b. intermarry with its inhabitants.
   c. militarily divide and conquer the land.
   d. establish the tribes as governors over the inhabitants.

3. The period between the Testaments is called the "silent era" because

   a. no one recorded Jewish history.
   b. the historical records were destroyed by fire.
   c. God's written revelation ceased.
   d. all prophecy had been fulfilled.

4. King Saul's kingdom and throne did not endure because

   a. Saul had no heir.
   b. Samuel did not approve of Saul.
   c. Saul disobeyed the word of the Lord.
   d. Saul was overthrown by the tribe of Judah.

5. The period when the Israelites spent seventy years as captives in a foreign land is called the time of the

   a. exodus.
   b. judges.
   c. kingdom.
   d. exile.

6. The event completing the Israelite deliverance from Egypt was

   a. the parting of the Red Sea.
   b. Moses' retrieval of the bones of Joseph.
   c. The death of the first-born.
   d. Pharaoh's belief in the God of the Hebrews.

7. The period of the judges was dominated by

   a. seven good kings and seven bad kings.
   b. seven cycles of sin, servitude, repentance, deliverance, and freedom.
   c. seven outstanding judges.
   d. seven years of plenty, seven years of famine.

8. The Exile for the Jews ended when

   a. a royal decree permitted the Jews to return to Jerusalem.
   b. the Egyptians rescued the Jews.
   c. the Queen of Persia, a Jewess, won her people's freedom.
   d. the Jews overthrew the Persians.

9. The story *not* marked by sin and compromise is that of

   a. Benjamin's capture of the daughters of Shiloh.
   b. Abimelech, the "Bramble" king.
   c. Eli's sons.
   d. Ruth.

10. His family's lineage in a foreign country was preserved by

    a. Judah.
    b. Joseph.
    c. Benjamin.
    d. Simeon.

11. The fall of man occurred when

    a. God created the woman.
    b. Adam named Eve.

c. Adam and Eve disobeyed God.

d. The serpent entered Eden.

12. The tribe that received "cities" rather than portions of land in the Promised Land was

a. Judah.

b. Levi.

c. Benjamin.

d. Asher.

13. The rebuilding of the temple was supervised by

a. Esther.

b. Zerubbabel.

c. Ezra.

d. Nehemiah.

14. During the "silent era" in Jewish history there occurred

a. construction of Herod's temple.

b. development of the Sadducees and the Pharisees.

c. completion of the Septuagint.

d. all of the above

15. Prompting the tribes of Israel to demand a king was

a. a desire to be like the nations around them.

b. disunity among the tribes.

c. the Philistine's capture of the ark.

d. Eli's dream.

16. While the Jews were in exile, the Babylonians were conquered by

a. the Assyrians.

b. the Egyptians.

c. the Medo-Persians.

d. none of the above.

17. As consequence to the fall of man,

a. man and Satan became enemies.

  b. childbirth entailed pain.
  c. death ended life.
  d. all of the above

18. At Moses' birth, the status of the Hebrew people was that of

  a. a well organized military force.
  b. a seafaring people.
  c. a densely populated slave community.
  d. a guild of tradesmen.

19. The "father of the nation of Israel" was

  a. Isaac.
  b. David.
  c. Jacob.
  d. Moses.

20. The Israelites sinned during the period of the judges by

  a. worshiping Canaanite gods.
  b. intermarrying with the Canaanites.
  c. failing to drive out the Canaanites.
  d. all of the above.

21. The Flood occurred because

  a. the earth became overpopulated.
  b. the Lord saw the wickedness of man.
  c. the Lord could not find ten righteous men.
  d. the ground was unproductive.

22. The book that sets forth God's "blessings" on Israel for obedience and "curses" for disobedience is

  a. Exodus.
  b. Numbers.
  c. Leviticus.
  d. Deuteronomy.

23. Abraham's first recorded act of faith was

  a. leaving Ur of the Chaldeans.

b. separating himself from Lot.
c. naming Hagar's child Ishmael.
d. honoring Melchizedek.

24. Surviving the fall of Jericho was/were

    a. Agag.
    b. Rahab's household.
    c. the Gibeonites.
    d. no one.

25. God communicated with His people during the kingdom period through the office of

    a. priest.
    b. scribe.
    c. judge.
    d. prophet.

26. During the exile the Jews were

    a. murdered.
    b. resettled in Rome.
    c. absorbed into the culture.
    d. sold to the Assyrians.

27. The event preceding the actual Exodus was

    a. Pentecost.
    b. the Feast of Harvest.
    c. the Feast of Ingathering.
    d. Passover.

28. The Persians were conquered by the

    a. Romans.
    b. Greeks.
    c. Jews.
    d. Egyptians.

29. Circumcision was

    a. a sign of the Abrahamic covenant.

b. a child's weaning feast.

c. marrying a widow to protect her dead husband's lineage.

d. separating grain from straw.

30. The tribes comprising the Southern Kingdom of Israel were

a. Manasseh and Ephraim.

b. Simeon, Judah, Benjamin, and Ephraim.

c. Judah and Benjamin.

d. Manasseh, Ephraim, Zebulun, and Naphtali.

31. At Mount Sinai Moses received

a. the Ten Commandments.

b. laws to govern Israel.

c. plans for the tabernacle.

d. all of the above.

32. After Solomon's death the fate of the kingdom was that

a. Civil War left two distinct divisions.

b. peace reigned for forty years.

c. the armies of Egypt attacked.

d. Assyria dissolved the kingdom.

33. During the period of the Judges Israel was *not* oppressed by

a. Philistia.

b. Egypt.

c. Midian.

d. Canaan.

34. The Scriptures were taught to the returning exiles by

a. Zerubbabel.

b. Nehemiah.

c. Sanballat.

d. Ezra.

35. The unique characteristic distinguishing Adam and Eve from the rest of Creation was that

    a. God created them first.
    b. God created them to reproduce.
    c. God created them all-knowing.
    d. God created them in His image.

36. The Old Testament event most often cited as evidence of God's redemptive power toward Israel is

    a. the Exodus from Egypt.
    b. the return from the Exile.
    c. the defeat of the Assyrian army.
    d. the fall of Jericho.

37. The sin Ezra found prevalent among the leaders of Israel was

    a. they did not keep the Sabbath.
    b. they worshiped Samaritan gods.
    c. they intermarried with heathen women.
    d. they did not give tithes to the Levites.

38. The Israelites wandered in the desert for forty years because

    a. they demanded meat instead of manna.
    b. they murmured against Moses and Aaron.
    c. they demanded fresh water.
    d. they rebelled against God at Kadesh-Barnea.

39. A result of the building of the Tower of Babel was that

    a. nations were established.
    b. the earth would never again be destroyed by water.
    c. Seth was born.
    d. Eden was closed to man.

40. In 722 B.C., the Northern Kingdom of Israel was conquered by

    a. the Egyptians.

b. the Assyrians.
c. the Babylonians.
d. the Persians.

41. A judge in Israel was

a. a traveling Levite who sold his services to local tribes.
b. the high priest.
c. a religious/political/military leader raised up by God.
d. a seer.

42. Living in Babylon and encouraging the exiles were

a. Amos and Hosea.
b. Jonah and Nahum.
c. Ezekiel and Daniel.
d. Haggai and Malachi.

43. The best description of the progress of the conquest at the time of Joshua's death is that

a. the Israelites alone occupied the Promised Land.
b. the Israelites co-existed with the Canaanites.
c. the Israelites were driven east of the Jordan.
d. the Israelites were taken captive by the Assyrians.

44. God rejected Cain's offering of

a. the fruit of the ground.
b. the firstlings of the cattle.
c. a mixture of spices.
d. none of the above.

45. The miracle providing the Israelites an easy entrance into the Promised Land was

a. the fall of Jericho.
b. a supply of "sweet water."
c. the parting of the Jordan.
d. the sun's standing still.

46. God's personal name, Jehovah was first revealed to the nation of Israel in the book of

 a. Genesis.
 b. Deuteronomy.
 c. 1 Samuel.
 d. none of the above.

47. The number of righteous kings governing the Northern Kingdom was

 a. none.
 b. eight.
 c. three.
 d. twelve.

48. The "child of promise" was

 a. Jacob.
 b. Samson.
 c. Samuel.
 d. Isaac.

49. David's contribution to the kingdom of Israel was that

 a. he consolidated the tribes and unified the nation.
 b. he bridged the period between the judges and the kingdom.
 c. he brought unsurpassed economic development.
 d. he made lasting treaties with the Queen of Sheba.

50. Privileged to set foot in the Promised Land was/were

 a. Moses.
 b. twelve spies.
 c. Aaron and Miriam.
 d. all of the above.

Answers

1. (b) A patriarch was a progenitor, an ancestor in the direct line of descent. Abraham, Isaac, and Jacob were considered the patriarchs of the Old Testament. The New Testament, how-

ever, included David (Acts 2:29) and Jacob's twelve sons (Acts 7:8–9).

2. (c.) Even though the siege of Jericho, Israel's first battle in the Promised Land, was unorthodox, chapters 7–12 of Joshua indicate that Israel's conquest of Canaan was a series of military operations. The army swept across central Canaan, subdued its southern territory, and then focused its attack on northern Canaan. Treaties, intermarriages, and feudal holdings were never a part of the Conquest strategy. In fact, Deuteronomy (7 and 20) clearly prohibited such tactics.

3. (c.) From Malachi to the birth of Christ God's written revelation ceased. There was no prophecy to record. Yet, in spite of the term *silent*, the four hundred years was an extremely active period in Jewish history (see answer 14).

4. (c.) Long before King Saul ever met David, God ordered the king to destroy the Amalekites (1 Samuel 15:1–3). Saul disobeyed, and his kingdom was transferred to "your neighbor who is better than you." (1 Samuel 15:28). Although Saul spent much of his life trying to assassinate David, the king did not actually know the name of the "neighbor" until the evening before his own death (1 Samuel 28:17).

5. (d.) The exile was seventy years. The number was not arbitrarily chosen. Seventy represented the number of years the nation had not allowed the land to enjoy its Sabbath rest (2 Chronicles 36:21; Leviticus 25:1–7; 26:34–35).

6. (a.) At the Red Sea, God graphically divided His people from their captors (Exodus 14:10–31). When Egypt's army drowned, the fledgling nation of Israel was free to travel to the Promised Land.

7. (b.) Judges is a chronicle of sin and its consequences. Seven times the Israelites cycled through phases of sin, servitude, repentance, deliverance, and freedom. Judges 2:11–19 succinctly summarizes the period.

8. (a.) " . . . the LORD stirred up the spirit of Cyrus king of Persia, so that he sent a proclamation throughout all his kingdom . . . saying . . . , 'The Lord, the God of heaven, has given me all the kingdoms of the earth, and He has appointed me to build Him a house in Jerusalem which is in Judah. Whoever there is among you of all His people, may his God be with him!

Let him go up to Jerusalem which is in Judah, and rebuild the house of the Lord . . . " (Ezra 1:1–3).

9. (d.) In the period of the judges, only the story of Ruth glistens as an example of faith and trust in the promises of God. Ruth's redemption by Boaz foreshadows the redemptive work of Christ for men who believe in God and order their lives accordingly.

10. (b.) The relationship that Joseph and his brothers had enjoyed in Egypt while their father was alive was threatened when Jacob died. Joseph's reassurance to his guilt-ridden brothers is one of the most godly examples of forgiveness in the Old Testament: "But as for you, you meant evil against me; but God meant it for good, in order to bring it about as it is this day, to save many people alive. . . . I will provide for you and your little ones" (Genesis 50:20–21).

11. (c.) The fall of man occurred when both Adam and Eve disobeyed God. Adam did not react to Eve's "fallen" condition until after he himself had sinned (Genesis 3:6–7).

12. (b.) While the inheritance of the Levites was the Lord Himself and service in the tabernacle (Numbers 18:20–21), the men were apportioned cities and pasture land in the Promised Land as Moses commanded (Numbers 35:1–5). The cities were spread throughout the land to allow the Levites to minister.

13. (b.) Zerubbabel, born in exile of the Davidic line, led the first wave of returning captives (nearly fifty thousand people) to Jerusalem. Zerubbabel and the high priest, Jeshua, supervised the restoration activities of the temple, a project which took more than two decades to complete (Ezra 4 and 5). Because of his dedication, the building was commonly referred to as "Zerubbabel's" temple.

14. (d.) During the Babylonian captivity, the Hebrew language began to diminish in importance. As the Jews were scattered throughout the Mediterranean area and as Greek became the common language, there was an urgent need for a Bible for Greek-speaking Jews. The Jewish community in Alexandria urged the king of Egypt (Ptolemy Philadelphus III?) to commission a Greek translation of the Bible for his library. The Septuagint (LXX), produced around 250–200 B.C., met the immediate need for Greek-speaking Jews. Later, it provided Christians

with the Old Testament written in a familiar language. The Septuagint set the precedent for Bible translation.

The Pharisees and the Sadducees developed around the time of Ezra. The Pharisees believed in the historic doctrines of Judaism. However, they emphasized keeping the law and created a rigid set of restrictions to prevent people from breaking the law. Their burdensome and joyless religion was called "legalism."

The Sadducees limited the canon to the writings of Moses, opposed legalism, and did not believe in judgment or an afterlife. Although they were religious leaders and priests, their world view was colored by Greek philosophy, liberal theology, and practical economics. Sadducees were generally wealthy, aristocratic men, the movers and shakers of the ancient Jewish world.

When Persia fell to Greece and Jerusalem came under the control of the Seleucids around 175 B.C., Antiochus Epiphanes worked to eradicate the Jewish faith. The temple was plundered and desecrated. Rome subsequently conquered the Greek Empire and Pompey captured Jerusalem. In 37 B.C. Herod the Great (and greatly deranged!) became king of Judea and Samaria. To gain favor with the Jews, Herod razed the original temple site and constructed "Herod's" temple (c.20–10 B.C.). Herod added the Courts of the Gentiles, the Women, and the Priests. The Court of the Gentiles became an ancient version of Wall Street, a place for commerce. Many important events in Jesus' life occurred around Herod's temple.

15. (a.) The elders of Israel offered feeble reasons for wanting a king, but their statement in 1 Samuel 8:19–20 is most telling: "We will have a king over us, that we also may be like all the nations." The request threw Samuel, the prophet-priest, into morbid depression, but Deuteronomy 17:14–20 had anticipated and addressed the moment.

16. (c.) The Medo-Persian army, commanded by Cyrus and led by Ugbaru, captured Babylon the night of October 12, 539 B.C., just as prophesied in chapter 5 of Daniel.

17. (d.) In Genesis 3 God judged all three participants in the "garden intrigue." To Satan, God decreed enmity and final destruction by the descendants of Eve. To Eve, He mandated

pain in childbirth and subservience to Adam. To Adam, God pledged toil and death.

18. (c.) The Egyptians, awed by the Israelites' fertility, subjected them to rigorous labor (Exodus 1:1–14). The Jews became slaves and lived in a clearly defined community close to the Nile. Pharaoh's daughter knew exactly where to find a wet nurse for the infant Moses (Exodus 2:1–10).

19. (c.) Jacob fathered the twelve men whose offsprings became the nation of Israel. Jacob's boys were conceived by four different women.

20. (d.) Israel did it all! The nation's sins stemmed from disobedience to God's Word as clearly called out in Deuteronomy 7 and 20.

21. (b.) The Flood was a judgment on the wickedness of man (Genesis 6:5, 12–13, 17).

22. (d.) Deuteronomy, also called the book of Remembrances, recounts God's gracious dealings with Israel, the nation's past failures, and the consequences which resulted. Moses reminds Israel that its future depends on the nation's relationship with God. In Deuteronomy God offers a clear choice: blessings for obedience or curses for disobedience.

23. (a.) Abraham left Ur! "By faith Abraham, when he was called, obeyed by going out to a place which he was to receive for an inheritance; and he went out, not knowing where he was going" (Hebrews 11:8).

24. (b.) Rahab's faith delivered her and her household from the fall of Jericho. This remarkable woman is listed in Hebrews 11:31 as a "hero" of the faith and in Matthew 1:5 as one of the ancestors of Jesus.

25. (d.) During the kingdom period, God communicated through the prophets. A prophet was a man called by God to remind the nation that: (1) God was in control of history; (2) sin required repentance; (3) society reflected a nation's righteousness; (4) in judgment there was hope; and (5) Israel's future was tied to the Messiah.

26. (c.) The Jews were generally absorbed into the culture. Babylon took captives at three different times over a nineteen-year period. Daniel and other aristocrats were the first exiles in 605 B.C. Ezekiel and ten thousand additional Israelites were

taken in 597. The Jews who survived the siege of Jerusalem were deported in 586. From Ezekiel and Esther it appears that the Jews congregated in communities, retained their national identity, and enjoyed a certain degree of freedom. When given the opportunity to return to Jerusalem in 538, only fifty thousand exiles accompanied Zerubbabel.

27. (d.) The first Passover was an act of faith. Blood from the Passover lamb was smeared on Jewish doorposts to preserve the firstborn from the last plague on Egypt. The Passover celebration became one of Israel's three national feasts (Exodus 12:1–24, 42; 23:14–17).

28. (b.) The Greeks, led by Alexander the Great, conquered Persia and ushered in the Hellenic era (331–167 B.C.). Under Alexander the Jews generally prospered. When the king died, the Syrian division of the Greek Empire ruled the Jews. Under the Syrians times were hard for Israel.

29. (a.) All Jewish males were circumcised as a sign of the Abrahamic covenant (Genesis 17:9–15). The procedure generally took place on the eighth day after a child's birth. However, during the wilderness period, the practice was not followed and the generation which entered the Promised Land had to be circumcised (Joshua 5:2–8).

30. (c.) After Solomon's death, his son Rehoboam attempted to maintain the kingdom, but the ten northern tribes rebelled. Only Judah and Benjamin continued under Davidic rule. The two tribes became known as the Southern Kingdom and Jerusalem remained their capital. Note that adherence to tribal territories was not strictly followed during the kingdom era and that Jerusalem, because of its prominence, probably contained some representation from all the tribes.)

31. (d.) At Sinai Moses received the Ten Commandments, the laws for governing the nation, and blueprints for the tabernacle (Exodus 20–40).

32. (a.) Because of Solomon's disobedience, the kingdom was divided during the reign of his son Rehoboam. The seeds for its destruction, however, were sown while Solomon still lived. The scenario unfolds in 1 Kings 11–12.

33. (b.) The Egyptians hovered along the coastal areas that the tribes had not claimed during the Conquest. The Egyptians

were seafarers and paid little attention to the Israelites who occupied the hill country. Under God's direction, Shagmar and Samson squelched the Philistines, Gideon routed the Midianites, and Deborah outwitted the Canaanites.

34. (d.) Ezra the teacher/priest instructed the returning exiles in the law of the Lord (Ezra 7:10). "Governor" Nehemiah recounted how Ezra's leadership led to spiritual revival in Israel (Nehemiah 8).

35. (d.) "So God created man in His own image, in the image of God He created him; male and female He created them" (Genesis 1:27). No other part of Creation was so imprinted by the Creator.

36. (a.) Israel's Exodus was a benchmark. God demonstrated His power over the Egyptians' gods, but He also assembled a nation from slaves and sustained His redeemed people for forty years.

37. (c.) When Ezra learned that Israel's leadership had intermarried with heathen women, he sought God's forgiveness through confession and intercessory prayer. Then Ezra and several other leaders determined to settle the complex matter and judged the marriages on an individual basis.

38. (d.) Sending spies to scout out Canaan was God's plan not Moses' idea. Kadesh-Barnea provided the opportunity for the "redeemed" from Egypt, those who had witnessed countless miracles on their behalf, to step out in faith and claim the land promised to their fathers. Israel's rebellion at Kadesh-Barnea resulted in judgment. "According to the number of the days in which you spied out the land, forty days, for each day you shall bear your guilt one year, namely forty years, and you shall know My rejection" (Numbers 14:34).

39. (a.) As a result of the building of the Tower of Babel, language was confounded and the people were scattered over the earth. Out of the nations that formed, God selected Israel to be the people from which "all the families of the earth shall be blessed" (Genesis 12:1-3).

40. (b.) In 722 B.C. Sargon II, king of Assyria, carried off the inhabitants of the northern Kingdom and sent Assyrian "strangers" to fill the cities of Israel, as Hosea and Amos had prophesied.

41. (c.) A judge was a multitalented leader raised up by God to free the tribes from oppression, administer justice, and/or steer the nation toward righteousness. Most judges performed all three functions and served continuously from the time of their call until their death (Judges 2:16–19). Samuel was a judge from the tribe of Levi, but judges were also selected from other tribes. Othniel represented Judah, Ehud was from Benjamin, and Samson belonged to the tribe of Dan.

42. (c.) Ezekiel and Daniel encouraged the captives at different times during the Exile. For more than ten years, Ezekiel wrote to the skeptical exiles in Babylon, who did not believe Jerusalem would fall. They were attentive, however, when Jerusalem was destroyed in 586. Ezekiel's later prophecies offered Israel hope for future restoration. Daniel's writings demonstrated how a true son of Israel should live. Daniel prayed, trusted God in all circumstances, and lived a godly life. The prophet explained the "times of the Gentiles," affirmed God's control over world leaders, and reminded the captives of God's covenant relationship with them.

43. (b.) By the time Joshua died, the initial phase of the Conquest was complete, but the Canaanitish nations had not been driven entirely from the land. The tribes still had a lot of "mopping up" to do. "See, I have apportioned to you these nations which remain as an inheritance for your tribes, with all the nations which I have cut off, from the Jordan even to the Great Sea toward the setting of the sun. And the Lord your God, He shall thrust them out from before you" (Joshua 23:4–5).

44. (a.) God rejected the fruit of the ground as an offering (Genesis 4:3–5); God did not reject Cain. When Cain understood what pleased God, it was well within his power to duplicate Abel's offering, but Cain chose not to do so. Since Cain could not strike out at God, he struck Abel, the one who had pleased God. The name *Cain* means "fabrication."

45. (c.) The parting of the Red Sea opened the Israelite's "wilderness" period and the parting of the Jordan River closed it. The miracle was all the more astounding since the Jews entered the Promised Land during barley harvest, a time when the Jordan normally overflowed (Joshua 3:14–15). Joshua re-

corded the precise day, "the tenth [day] of the first month" (4:19). Exactly forty years earlier, on the tenth day of the first month, Israel's "exodus generation" had prepared its lamb for the first Passover feast (Exodus 12:3).

46. (d.) God revealed His personal name to Moses in Exodus 3:13–15. The name was given to underwrite Moses' authority and to identify the people with "the Lord, the God of your fathers, the God of Abraham, the God of Isaac, and the God of Jacob."

47. (a.) Nineteen kings, representing nine dynasties, ruled the northern kingdom for two hundred years. Not one of the nineteen was righteous before God.

48. (d.) Although there were prophecies concerning the births of Jacob, Samson, and Samuel, Isaac was called the "child of promise" (Genesis 17:15–19; 21:1–8; Galatians 4:23, 28).

49. (a.) David ably fashioned the tribes into a kingdom. He secured the land, assembled the trusted Cherethites and Pelethites, and consolidated military power under Joab. David organized worship under Zadok, established his sons as ministers, and officially documented his royal proceedings. David made Jerusalem the nation's capital.

50. (b.) Of the original "exodus generation" only the spies set foot in the Promised Land. Joshua and Caleb were among the spies.

FOUR

THE POETICAL BOOKS

HAS A METAPHOR EVER SAVED A SOUL?

> "The time has come," the Walrus said,
> "To talk of many things:
> Of shoes—and ships—and sealing wax—
> Of cabbages—and kings—
> And why the sea is boiling hot—
> And whether pigs have wings."
>
> —Lewis Carroll, "The Walrus and the Carpenter"

By the time the walrus quotes his famous lines, we are well along in the bizarre beach walk. Not only are "The Walrus and the Carpenter" enjoying the moon and sun-lit night, but a host of breathless, young oysters are merrily following behind, unaware that something is about to alter their pleasant evening.

So, too, it is with *Test Your Christian Literacy*. We have meandered through biblical geography. We have surveyed the Bible. We have marched through Old Testament history and while we, like the little oysters, are catching our breaths, the structure of the Bible introduces something unexpected. The time has come to talk poetry.

Poetry! The word arouses cries of panic. Like the oysters, we may shout: "What a dismal thing to do!" But, our protests are likely to be modern: "Poetry is awful!" "Nobody talks like that anymore."

69

Like it or not, poetry is an important part of the Bible. What's more, it is a very popular part, because the Old Testament section most often included with the New Testament (or published alone) is the Psalms. And, the Psalms are poetry.

There are five poetical books in the Bible: Job, Psalms, Proverbs, Ecclesiastes, and the Song of Solomon. But, poetry is not limited to the poetical books. Elements of poetry appear in the histories, prophecies, and the epistles as well.

Americans expect poetry to have form, regular rhyme, and cadence. Biblical poetry, however, is a verse form characterized by a balance of thought patterns.

How is this done? Through figurative language. Figures of speech—similes and metaphors, apostrophes and personification—are just a few of the technical building blocks of poetry. Each time a poet uses figurative language well, the reader benefits. Isaiah could have encouraged the captives with: "The Lord will help you." Instead, he wrote:

> . . . those who wait for the Lord
> Will gain new strength;
> They will mount up with wings like eagles,
> They will run and not get tired,
> They will walk and not become weary.

Isaiah's language is vivid. We read it and hope surges.

There is a widespread tendency today to dismiss figures of speech as "too intellectual" and not really that important. After all, has a metaphor ever saved a soul?

The answer is a resounding yes. Figures of speech force readers to think! Jesus constantly perplexed the disciples with His figurative language, e.g., Matthew 13:10–17; John 16:25–29. The figures caused the apostles to ask questions and provided opportunities for teaching.

Figures of speech enrich our biblical understanding by illustrating spiritual principles through the use of concrete examples. Is the Lord your shepherd? Your rock? Your refuge? Your shield? Your banner? Then, the power of a metaphor nourishes your soul.

In addition to examining the figures of speech used by the poets, the following test also focuses on the period and content of their books, some key verses, and the poets themselves.

Questions

1. A proverb is
   a. a short, memorable statement of truth.
   b. a personal letter.
   c. a complaint.
   d. a list of things to avoid.

2. The book that is a collection of songs and hymns is
   a. Job.
   b. Psalms.
   c. Proverbs.
   d. Song of Solomon.

3. "The fear of the Lord is the beginning of _____."
   a. prosperity.
   b. joy.
   c. sacrifice.
   d. wisdom.

4. ". . . there is a time for every event under heaven—a time to give birth, and a time to die; a time to plant, and a time to uproot what is planted." These verses are found in
   a. Psalms.
   b. Proverbs.
   c. Ecclesiastes.
   d. Song of Solomon.

5. "The Preacher" or "the Teacher" appears in
   a. Job.
   b. Proverbs.
   c. Song of Solomon.
   d. Ecclesiastes.

6. The type of poetry found in Proverbs is
   a. lyric poetry.
   b. instructional poetry.
   c. dramatic poetry.
   d. none of the above.

7. The book of Psalms contains _____ psalms.
   a. 50
   b. 100
   c. 150
   d. 3000

8. Hebrew poetry matches ideas in a verse form called
   a. parallelism.
   b. personification.
   c. allusion.
   d. satire.

9. "I am my beloved's, and his desire is toward me." This key verse appears in
   a. Job.
   b. Ecclesiastes.
   c. Song of Solomon.
   d. Psalms.

10. God reviews His actions in Creation in
    a. Ecclesiastes.
    b. Proverbs.
    c. Song of Solomon.
    d. Job.

11. God permitted Job to be tested by
    a. Satan.
    b. Gabriel.
    c. a neighboring king.
    d. the high priest.

12. The opening passage of Psalm 1 is:

    a. "Lord, our Lord, how majestic is Thy name in all the earth."

    b. "How blessed is the man who does not walk in the counsel of the wicked . . . But his delight is in the law of the Lord."

    c. "The Lord is my shepherd, I shall not want."

    d. "Unless the Lord builds the house, they labor in vain who build it."

13. Eliphaz, Bildad, Zophar, and Elihu were

    a. Job's sons.
    b. Solomon's servants.
    c. Job's friends.
    d. minor psalmists.

14. Hebrew poets used _____ to paint mental word pictures in the reader's mind.

    a. similes
    b. metaphors
    c. personification
    d. all of the above

15. "Train up a _____ in the way he should go, even when he is old he will not depart from it."

    a. child
    b. worker
    c. disciple
    d. none of the above

16. Excluding David, the most psalms were written by

    a. Solomon.
    b. Asaph.
    c. Moses.
    d. Heman.

17. The book emphasizing "vanity" and "under the sun" was

    a. Psalms.
    b. Job.
    c. Ecclesiastes.
    d. Song of Solomon.

18. Job's peace of mind was restored by

    a. Job's wife.
    b. God Himself.
    c. a wandering prophet.
    d. Job's son.

19. "Haughty eyes, a lying tongue, and hands that shed inno-
    cent blood, a heart that devises wicked plans, feet that run
    rapidly to evil, a false witness who utters lies, and one who
    spreads strife among brothers." The preceding verses col-
    lectively describe

    a. the sins of Achan.
    b. things God hates.
    c. false teachers.
    d. Doeg's slaughter of the priests.

20. Worship is the central theme in

    a. Ecclesiastes.
    b. Job.
    c. Psalms.
    d. Proverbs.

21. "Why are you in despair, O my soul?" As in this quotation,
    an address to someone or something absent as though he
    (it) were present is called

    a. a simile.
    b. an apostrophe.
    c. an allusion.
    d. a pun.

22. Ecclesiastes was written by

    a. Solomon.
    b. Samuel.
    c. David.
    d. Asaph.

23. The *last* verse of the Twenty-third Psalm is:

    a. "Let the words of my mouth and the meditation of my heart be acceptable in Thy sight, O Lord, my rock and my redeemer."

    b. "So we Thy people and the sheep of Thy pasture will give thanks to Thee forever; to all generations we will tell of Thy praise.

    c. "O Lord, our Lord, how majestic is Thy name in all the earth!"

    d. "Surely goodness and lovingkindness will follow me all the days of my life, and I will dwell in the house of the Lord forever."

24. The book which encourages its readers to be godly decision-makers, especially about the practical matters of life is

    a. Psalms.
    b. Job.
    c. Song of Solomon.
    d. Proverbs.

25. An example of dramatic poetry is

    a. Psalm 119.
    b. Job.
    c. Proverbs.
    d. Ecclesiastes.

26. "The stone which the builders rejected has become the chief cornerstone." This passage (Psalm 118:22) is a prophecy concerning

    a. Herod the Great.

b. Zerubbabel.

c. Solomon.

d. Jesus.

27. "As the deer pants for the water brooks, so my soul pants for Thee, O God" is an example of a

a. simile.

b. metaphor.

c. hyperbole.

d. personification.

28. Job is believed to take place about the time of the

a. kingdom.

b. Conquest.

c. patriarchs.

d. Exile.

29. The verse, "If my land cries out against me, and its furrows weep together," is an example of

a. a simile.

b. an apostrophe.

c. personification.

d. a rhetorical question.

30. The subject of Psalm 119 is

a. God's word.

b. David's sin with Bathsheba.

c. old age.

d. the King of glory coming to Zion.

31. The kind of poetry that concentrates on the thoughts and feelings of the writer is known as

a. instructional poetry.

b. lyric poetry.

c. dramatic poetry.

d. none of the above.

32. *Hallelujah* means

    a. "pause for silence."
    b. "amen."
    c. "praise ye the Lord."
    d. "clap your hands."

33. At the beginning of the book, Job was

    a. a prophet who has been sent to Nineveh.
    b. a godly, prosperous man.
    c. a foolish man who refuses hospitality to a brother.
    d. the King of Salem.

34. "My tears have been my food day and night" is a hyperbole, which is a

    a. pun.
    b. rhetorical question.
    c. deliberate exaggeration for the sake of effect.
    d. lament.

35. The central character of Ecclesiastes found lasting satisfaction in

    a. nothing.
    b. a long life.
    c. riches, wealth, and honor.
    d. his work.

36. The lady whose worth is "far above jewels," who is clothed with "strength and dignity," whose "children rise up and bless her" is found in

    a. Song of Solomon.
    b. Proverbs.
    c. Job.
    d. Ecclesiastes.

37. "By the rivers of Babylon, there we sat down and wept, when we remembered Zion."

    The psalmist in the passage above wept because

a. King David had died.
b. Israel was in captivity.
c. Absalom had seized the Kingdom.
d. the Philistines had captured the ark of God.

38. The author of most of the Proverbs was

a. an unnamed writer.
b. Moses.
c. David.
d. Solomon.

39. An acrostic is

a. a poem where verses or sections begin with successive
   letters of the Hebrew alphabet.
b. a musical instrument used in the temple.
c. an Old Testament greeting.
d. a poem which calls down curses on an enemy.

40. "_____ exalts a nation but sin is a disgrace to any people."

a. Righteousness
b. Prosperity
c. Peace
d. Mercy

41. A country maid who works a vineyard is a central character
in

a. Job.
b. Proverbs 31.
c. Ecclesiastes.
d. Song of Solomon.

42. Select the following verse that contains a metaphor.

a. "Thy word is a lamp to my feet, and a light to my path."
b. "Your stature is like a palm tree."
c. "What is man, that Thou dost take thought of him?"
d. "Let the rivers clap their hands; let the mountains sing
   together for joy."

43. The concluding advice of Ecclesiastes is:

    a. "The Almighty—we cannot find Him; He is exalted in power."

    b. "Consider the work of God, for who is able to straighten what He has bent?"

    c. "Do not be hasty in word or impulsive in thought to bring up a matter in the presence of God. . . . therefore let your words be few."

    d. "Fear God and keep His commandments."

44. "So teach us to number our days,
    That we may present to Thee a heart of wisdom."

    The above passage, from what is believed to be the oldest psalm, was written by

    a. David.
    b. Solomon.
    c. Moses.
    d. Asaph.

45. To be "sovereign" means
    a. all-knowing.
    b. unchanging.
    c. unable to tolerate sin.
    d. totally in control.

46. The book containing both the longest and the shortest chapters in the Old Testament is
    a. Job.
    b. Psalms.
    c. Proverbs.
    d. Ecclesiastes.

47. In the Song of Solomon, Solomon's role is
    a. a bridegroom.
    b. a ship's captain.

c. a horse trainer.
d. a warrior.

48. _____ defended himself with the verse: "Though He slay me, I will hope in Him."

a. David
b. Job
c. Solomon
d. Moses

49. "_____
And do not lean on your own understanding.
In all your ways acknowledge Him,
And He will make your paths straight."

The correct first line for the above passage is

a. "Honor the Lord from your wealth,"
b. "Trust in the Lord with all your heart,"
c. "Do not withhold good from those to whom it is due,"
d. "Do not let kindness and truth leave you,"

50. The last verse in the Psalms is:

a. "In peace I will both lie down and sleep, for Thou alone, O Lord, dost make me to dwell in safety."

b. "Let the words of my mouth and the meditation of my heart be acceptable in Thy sight, O Lord, my rock and my redeemer."

c. "Praise the Lord!"

d. "And do confirm for us the work of our hands; yes, confirm the work of our hands."

Answers

1. (a.) A proverb is an aphorism, a short saying that contains practical truth or guides for conduct. Rather than being simply a catchy little saying, the proverb is a major literary form used in Biblical poetry, the epistles, and the Gospels. The proverb is

brief. Its shortness is striking, lingering in memory. The proverb is profound. It blends verbal skill with human insight. The proverb simultaneously addresses a specific situation and makes a general observation, as Jesus does with the axiom: "No one can serve two masters" (Matthew 6:24).

2. (b.) *Psalms* means "songs." Originally, the psalms were the temple hymnbook. Many were accompanied by music. The songs were collected over several hundred years and eventually became known as the "Book of Praises."

3. (d.) "The fear of the Lord is the beginning of wisdom" (Proverbs 9:10). The verse captures the theme of Proverbs; the idea also occurs in Job 28:28, in Psalm 111:10, and in Proverbs 9:10. Proverbs is often called the "Book of Wisdom."

4. (c.) Ecclesiastes 3:1–2.

5. (d.) The preacher/teacher is the central figure in Ecclesiastes. Hebrew grammar indicates that the word *preacher/teacher* is a special title rather than a proper name. If it is a title, it is used of no other person in the Old Testament.

6. (b.) Proverbs, or maxims, are instructional (teaching) poetry. The modern reader often has the impression that Bible writers were "zapped" by the Holy Spirit and the words simply wrote themselves. The Preacher of Ecclesiastes dispels such a notion: "And moreover, because the Preacher was wise, he still taught the people knowledge; yes, he pondered and sought out and set in order many proverbs. The Preacher sought to find acceptable words; and what was written was upright—words of truth (Ecclesiastes 12:9–10). Thus the writer "worked" as the Holy Spirit "superintended" the writing.

7. (c.) There are 150 psalms.

8. (a.) Parallelism, the foundation of all Biblical poetry, is a verse form in which two or more lines form a pattern based on repetition, balance of thought, or grammar. Psalm 25:4 is a good example:

> Show me Your ways, O Lord;
> Teach me Your paths.

Psalm 25:4 is *synonymous* parallelism because the ideas presented in both lines are similar. Another form is *antithetic* parallelism, where the second line contrasts the first:

> My son, keep your father's command,
> And do not forsake the law of your mother.
>   (Proverbs 6:20)

A third form is *synthetic* parallelism, where the second line develops and completes the idea of the first line:

> The Lord is my shepherd,
> I shall not want.
>   (Psalm 23:1)

Parallelism also makes its way into prose, where the sentence, rather than the verse, is the unit of expression. Consider:

> The race is not to the swift,
> Nor the battle to the strong,
> Nor bread to the wise,
> Nor riches to men of understanding.
>   (Ecclesiastes 9:11)

9. (c.) The Song of Solomon describes the emotional and intimate aspects of marriage in a series of scenes, some of which are rather confusing without stage directions! The king is called "my beloved," and the bride is "my darling." The individual scenes reinforce the key verse (Song 7:10).

10. (d.) Job 38–41 magnificently sweeps through Creation in a way Genesis 1 never did. Genesis is journalism; Job is poetry! In Job we glimpse Divine creativity at work. It is worth struggling through the diatribes of Job 3–37 just to behold the majesty of God in 38–41.

11. (a.) Satan's assault on Job is a classic example of the roaring lion "prowling around" seeking someone to devour (1 Peter 5:8). Note carefully that God singled out Job on more than one occasion (Job 1:8; 2:3).

12. (b.) As a preview to the whole book of Psalms, Psalm 1 offers peace of mind, distinguishes between righteous and

wicked living, and focuses on the surety of God's word. These ideas permeate the remaining psalms.

13. (c.) Eliphaz, Bildad, Zophar, and Elihu were Job's friends. While their advice pushed Job toward self-righteousness, the men identified with Job's suffering. Eliphaz, Bildad, and Zophar came quickly and from great distances when they learned about Job's trouble, and the three spent several days quietly waiting for Job to regain his composure. Elihu, Job's much younger friend, deliberately postponed his visit, deferring to the "wisdom" of older men.

14. (d.) Like all bards, the Hebrew poets used figures of speech to convey their ideas. Figures commonly found in Scripture include the following: simile, metaphor, apostrophe, hyperbole, rhetorical question, and personification.

15. (a.) Proverbs 22:6.

16. (b.) Asaph is rarely acclaimed, but he wrote twelve psalms (Psalms 50 and 73–83) making him the number two contributor to the book. Before David brought the ark into Jerusalem, he "spoke to the chiefs of the Levites to appoint their relatives the singers, with instruments of music, harps, lyres, loud-sounding cymbals, to raise sounds of joy" (1 Chronicles 15:16). As a result, Asaph became one of Israel's first musical directors. Wasting no time, he wrote a thanksgiving psalm for the ark's arrival and played loud-sounding cymbals as accompaniment (1 Chronicles 16). Several of Asaph's descendants were prominent at critical times in Israel's history (1 Chronicles 25:1–2, 6, 9; 2 Chronicles 20:14; 29:13–14, 30; 35:15; Ezra 2:41; Nehemiah 11:17, 22–23; 12:35, 46; Isaiah 36:3, 22). Solomon, incidentally, authored Psalms 72 and 127. Moses wrote Psalm 90, and Heman composed Psalm 88.

17. (c.) *Vanity* and *under the sun* are the words of Ecclesiastes. Vanity and its variations are mentioned more than thirty-five times. "Under the sun" occurs nearly thirty times.

18. (b.) God restored Job's perspective with two discourses recorded in Job 38–41. God's first communication with Job left him speechless (Job 38:1–40:2). God's second statement (Job 40:6–41:34) left Job repentant, humbled by God's sovereignty (Job 42).

19. (b.) Proverbs 6:16–19 describe seven things which are an abomination to God.

20. (c.) Psalms is also called the "Book of Praises." Praise is the central element of worship. Nearly every psalm praises some aspect of God—His nature, His character, or His roles. Psalm 145, a psalm of David, characteristically concludes with the worshipful and focal verse:

> My mouth will speak the praise of the Lord;
> And all flesh will bless
> His holy name forever and ever.

21. (b.) An apostrophe addresses someone or something absent as though he (it) were present. The Psalms are filled with apostrophes: "Depart from me, all you who do iniquity" (Psalm 6:8); "Sing for joy in the Lord, O you righteous ones" (Psalm 33:1); and "Praise Him, sun and moon" (Psalm 148:3).

22. (a.) Internal evidence suggests that Solomon wrote Ecclesiastes. Ecclesiastes 1:1 identifies the writer as the "son of David," while Ecclesiastes 1:12–2:26 provides the reader with a short biographical sketch of the author. 1 Kings 4:29–34 further supports Solomon's authorship.

23. (d.) Psalm 23:6.

24. (d.) In Ecclesiastes, we wrestle with the meaning of life. In Job we confront the issue of suffering. In the Psalms we discover the words for worship, but in the Proverbs we get dawn-to-dark advice about our attitudes and conduct.

25. (b.) Job is dramatic poetry. Although the prologue and the epilogue of Job are written in fast-moving prose, the lengthy dialogue section (Job 3:1–42:6) is rich with figurative language about God's power, natural phenomena, and ancient legal reasoning. Another dramatic poem is the Song of Solomon.

26. (d.) The Psalms contain a number of prophetic verses, many about the coming Messiah. The New Testament leaves little doubt that the chief cornerstone was Jesus Christ (Matthew 21:42; Mark 12:10; Luke 20:17; Acts 4:11; Ephesians 2:20; 1 Peter 2:6–7). Psalm 118 was traditionally sung at the Passover

meal, and, therefore, was one of the very last songs Jesus heard before His Crucifixion.

27. (a.) This passage (Psalm 42:1) is a simile. The simile and the metaphor both compare two unlike objects. The simile uses the helping words *like* or *as*, while the metaphor boldly equates one thing with another, e.g., "The Lord is my shepherd" (Psalm 23:1).

28. (c.) There are several reasons why Job probably occurred during the time of the patriarchs. First, Job's wealth was reckoned in terms of livestock, which was the custom in the times of Abraham, Isaac, and Jacob (Genesis 13:2; 26:13–14; 30:43). Second, since Job lived 140 years after his affliction (Job 42:10,16), his total life covered 210 years, a life span similar to those of Abraham and Isaac (Genesis 25:7; 35:28). Third, Job's daughters received an inheritance along with their brothers (Job 42:15). Under the later Mosaic law, such a transaction would have been improbable (Numbers 27:1–8).

29. (c.) The land "crying" and furrows "weeping" are personification, a figure of speech which ascribes human qualities to inanimate objects. In the poet's world, "the trees of the field clap their hands" (Isaiah 55:12), the "mountains sing together for joy" (Psalm 98:8), and the "land cries out against me" (Job 31:38).

30. (a.) Psalm 119 is a collection of meditations about the importance of Scripture. The psalm contains ten synonyms for God's word: law, word, saying, commandment, statutes, judgment, precepts, testimony, way, and path. Nearly all of the Psalms' 176 verses contain one of these synonyms.

31. (b.) By using figurative language lyric poetry creates a mood. It was often set to music. In Psalm 38:1–2 we feel David's discomfort:

> O Lord, rebuke me not in Thy wrath;
> And chasten me not in Thy burning anger.
> For Thine arrows have sunk deep into me,
> And Thy hand has pressed down on me.

Lyric poetry is evocative. In the Song of Solomon (4:9) the lover's affection becomes almost hypnotic:

> You have made my heart beat
> faster, my sister, my bride;
> You have made my heart beat
> faster with a single glance of your eyes,

With a single strand of your necklace."

32. (c.) *Hallelujah* literally means "praise ye the Lord." Hallelujah sometimes punctuates the Psalms (104:35; 105:45; 116:19). At other times, it is used to both open and close the psalms (Psalm 106:1,48; 146:1,10; 147:1,20; 150:1,6). From the Hebrew word *hallel*, meaning "praise," come the Hallel Psalms (113–118) which were sung on special feast days, particularly at Passover. *Alleluia*, a Latin–Greek derivative, is actually a misspelling of the Hebrew word.

33. (b.) Job was a spiritual yuppie. He had everything. He feared God, fathered sons and daughters, and possessed enormous wealth (Job 1:1–5).

34. (c.) Hyperbole is a deliberate exaggeration for the sake of an effect. David could have simply said he was troubled, but, like a skilled poet, he chose the hyperbole: "My tears have been my food day and night" (Psalm 42:3).

35. (a.) With frankness the Preacher concludes: "I have seen all the works which have been done under the sun, and behold, all is vanity and striving after wind" (Ecclesiastes 1:14). He finds no lasting satisfaction in anything — not long life, riches, or work (Ecclesiastes 11:8–10; 5:10–14; 6:2; 2:11; 4:4).

36. (b.) Proverbs 31 paints a rare portrait of womanhood in the Old Testament. In an age where marriage primarily secured political/economic gain, King Lemuel extols the wife of noble character. This favorable public comment stands in contrast to the proverbs about the adulterous woman and the contentious wife (Proverbs 6; 7; 19:13; 21:9, 19).

37. (b.) Psalm 137, one of the later psalms, finds an exiled Israelite, lamenting: "How can we sing the Lord's song in a foreign land?" (Psalm 137:4). The psalmist's melancholy is reminiscent of Lamentations 1 and 2 where Jeremiah conducts a postmortem for the ravaged city of Jerusalem. The unnamed

author of Psalm 137 may have been well acquainted with Jeremiah's writings. He was well acquainted with captivity!

38. (d.) Proverbs was written mainly, but not exclusively, by King Solomon. Since Solomon was the wisest man of his day (1 Kings 4:29–31), it is fitting that he was the "chief aphorist." Solomon took his writing seriously (Ecclesiastes 12:9–10). However, his success or his production schedule caused him to lament: "be warned: the writing of many books is endless, and excessive devotion to books is wearying to the body" (Ecclesiastes 12:12). Scripture records approximately eight hundred of Solomon's three thousand proverbs (1 Kings 4:32).

39. (a.) An acrostic is a poem in which verses or sections begin with successive letters of the Hebrew alphabet. The writing about the "excellent woman" in Proverbs 31 and Psalms 9, 10, 25, 34, 37, 111, 119, and 145 are all acrostics or variations thereof. Psalm 119 is the most famous and most elaborate of the acrostic poems. Each of its twenty-two sections contains eight verses. The twenty-two sections correspond to the twenty-two letters of the Hebrew alphabet. The eight verses in each section begin with the same letter in the proper sequence of the Hebrew alphabet. For example, each of the eight verses in the first section begins with *aleph*, verses 9–16 all begin with *beth*, etc. Unfortunately, the artistic affect is lost on a non-Hebrew reading audience.

40. (a.) "Righteousness exalts a nation, but sin is a disgrace to any people" (Proverbs 14:34).

41. (d.) The "my darling" of the Song of Solomon is indeed a country maid who met the king while tending a vineyard. "My darling" was evidently beautiful in spite of her sunburned complexion. Solomon comments that among his queens, concubines, and maidens, she was "perfect" and "unique," an opinion shared by the entire harem (Song of Solomon 6:8–9).

42. (a.) The metaphor is: "Thy word is a lamp to my feet" (Psalm 119:105).

43. (d.) Once Solomon has stated and supported his philosophic observations about life, he concludes: "fear God and keep His commandments . . . . For God will bring every act to judgment, everything which is hidden, whether it is good or evil" (Ecclesiastes 12:13–14).

44. (c.) Moses' Psalm 90 is believed to be the oldest of the psalms. The poem extols God's sovereignty, defines "Divine time" in terms of human years, and offers insight about the brevity of life.

45. (d.) Job highlighted God's sovereignty. Sovereignty implies superiority in power, influence, and importance plus the ability to exert controlling influence over situations and people. No purpose of God is ever thwarted, stymied, or frustrated. God's sovereignty humbled Job:

> I know that Thou canst do all things,
> And that no purpose of Thine can be thwarted.
> (Job 42:2)

46. (b.) Psalm 119 with its 176 verses is the longest chapter in the Old Testament; Psalm 117 with two verses is the shortest.

47. (a.) Considering his seven hundred wives and three hundred concubines, it is not surprising to catch a quick glimpse of Solomon as a bridegroom and husband. Evidently Solomon's marriage to "my darling" came early in his reign, since he only had sixty wives and eighty concubines at this point (Song 6:8).

48. (b.) Job was sure God would exonerate him because of the brilliance of his legal arguments (13:3–28). His assumption was misguided, human optimism. Yet, Job never relinquished his basic trust in God.

49. (b.) Proverbs 3:5–6 begins: "Trust in the Lord with all your heart".

50. (c.) Psalms 146–150 are all praise psalms. Therefore, it is fitting that the last psalm ends with a *hallelujah* "Praise the Lord!"

FIVE

THE PROPHETICAL BOOKS

THERE'S NO TELLING WHAT GOES ON IN THE MIND of a seventeen-year-old boy who has been sent to prune a cherry tree, but the visions Robert Goddard saw in 1899 from a leafy perch in his grandmother's orchard impelled him through life. There, Goddard was smitten by an idea: "how wonderful it would be to make some device which had even the possibility of ascending to Mars!"

Not everyone was enthusiastic about his idea. His Harvard-educated cousin announced it couldn't be done, and Robert's father nicknamed him "the angel shooter." Nevertheless, space travel captivated the young man, and ten years later in 1909, Robert's sketchbook contained a half dozen pictures of space vehicles. In one drawing there is a winged "car" driven by "explosive jets of liquid hydrogen and liquid oxygen" and steered by "side-jets." The vehicle bears a striking resemblence to our modern space shuttle. Robert's drawings only earned him a media nickname: "the Moon Man."

More than two and a half decades after pruning the cherry tree, Robert, the rocket scientist, launched his first liquid-fueled missile on his Aunt Effie's farm. The rocket ascended to a height of forty-one feet and traveled from its launch pad to the cabbage patch, a distance of 184 feet. The flight lasted 2.5 seconds. Robert was elated, but one of his assistants felt he could have thrown a baseball farther.

A follow-up experiment in July 1929 exploded, causing such a local hullabaloo that the *Boston Globe* headlined: "Moon Rocket Man's Test Alarms Whole Countryside." Massachusetts was not ready for space travel and Robert was ordered to cease and desist.

Late in 1929 Charles Lindbergh, the famed aviator, persuaded philanthropist Daniel Guggenheim to underwrite Goddard's testing. Armed with his sketchbook and experiments, Goddard moved to New Mexico where the desert became the backdrop for his launches.

Little attention was paid to the rocket wizard in the United States, but Goddard's work infused life into the calculations of the rocket pioneers of Germany, who later migrated to America and undergirded its infant space program.

Robert Hutchings Goddard, the "angel shooter," died on August 10, 1945.

In July 1969, exactly forty years after Goddard's exploding projectile banned him from Boston and other parts of the Commonwealth, a rocket named *Apollo 11* winged its way to the moon. A *New York Times* editorial recalled the day the paper had ridiculed Goddard's rockets and apologized—posthumously.

Like the *New York Times*, there are moments in life when we simply have to say, "If I'd only known!" The future is hidden from men and nations. But it was not always so.

Israel was a nation who needed no diviners, for God provided the prophets to guide the nation into its tomorrows. The prophets were "foretellers" who recorded history in advance. This was a critical task, since Scripture based its authority on the reliability of its predictive messages. Consequently, the prophets, the prophetical books, and prophecy in general require our close attention.

The prophet was literally a spokesperson for God—an awesome "working relationship!" In addition to describing future events, the prophet clarified the present and sometimes explained the past. His messages contained specific details. Zechariah, for instance, foretold that Christ would be betrayed for thirty pieces of silver (Zechariah 11:12–13) and forsaken by His disciples (13:7). At times, through oracle or burden, dreams or visions, a prophet, such as Ezekiel, spoke of places and events totally foreign to his own experience.

The seventeen prophetical books of the Old Testament (Isaiah — Malachi) record God's thoughts and reactions, many times in His own words. These books reveal God's personality, His pleasure or displeasure, His judgments, and His pivotal utterances of hope. The prophetical books prove God's trustworthiness; they feature Him in the sovereign and strategic role of decision maker. Unlike the *New York Times*, God has never had to apologize.

The best reason for paying close attention to prophecy is Jesus Christ: "For the testimony of Jesus is the spirit of prophecy" (Revelation 19:10). What Genesis and the Old Testament saw dimly as promise, the New Testament and Revelation see sharply as Person. Fulfilled prophecy, the prophets, and the prophetical books are the events, the people, and the words through which Jesus comes sharply into focus in our day as King of Kings and Lord of Lords.

Questions

1. A prophet is characterized by his
   a. authority from God.
   b. appointment by God.
   c. communication from God.
   d. all of the above

2. A prophet shifted the message of his sixty-six chapters from judgment to hope with the words: "'Comfort, O comfort My people,' says your God." His name was
   a. Daniel.
   b. Isaiah.
   c. Jeremiah.
   d. Jonah.

3. The activity that was *not* a usual part of a prophet's ministry was
   a. exposing sin.

b. warning of God's judgment.

c. offering temple sacrifices.

d. proclaiming Messiah's coming.

4. The prophet who pouted when his listeners repented was

    a. Jonah.

    b. Amos.

    c. Obadiah.

    d. Micah.

5. The basis on which a prophet was labeled "major" or "minor" is that

    a. major prophets preached only to kings.

    b. the messages of major prophets were longer.

    c. the major prophets preached during the Exile.

    d. the messages of major prophets prompted quick repentance.

6. Two prophets strongly emphasized the phrase, the "day of the Lord." One was Joel; the other was

    a. Nahum.

    b. Micah.

    c. Haggai.

    d. Zephaniah.

7. The ultimate test of a prophet was that

    a. he must perform miracles.

    b. he must be a Levite.

    c. he must be 100 percent accurate.

    d. he must have hand-written a copy of the law.

8. Nahum called down judgment on Israel's enemy,

    a. Assyria.

    b. Egypt.

    c. Edom.

    d. Babylon.

9. In the list below the only one *not* a major prophet is

   a. Zephaniah.
   b. Jeremiah.
   c. Isaiah.
   d. Daniel.

10. "Though the fig tree should not blossom, and there be no fruit on the vines . . . yet I will exult in the Lord, I will rejoice in the God of my salvation."

    The passage cited above is the conclusion of the dismayed prophet

    a. Obadiah.
    b. Joel.
    c. Habakkuk.
    d. Micah.

11. Explaining the succession of world empires that would dominate Israel, Daniel interpreted the dream of

    a. the handwriting on the wall.
    b. the man dressed in linen.
    c. the great tree.
    d. the image of metal and clay.

12. As a "forthteller," a prophet

    a. proclaimed God's teaching to the people.
    b. took a Nazirite vow.
    c. predicted the future.
    d. encouraged other prophets.

13. Called to be a prophet before his birth, the man who foretold the length of Judah's exile in Babylon was

    a. Nahum.
    b. Ezekiel.
    c. Isaiah.
    d. Jeremiah.

14. The *first* recorded messianic prophecy in Scripture is

    a. "The scepter shall not depart from Judah, nor the ruler's staff from between his feet, until Shiloh comes . . . ."

    b. "And in you all the families of the earth shall be blessed."

    c. "And I will put enmity between you and the woman, and between your seed and her seed; He shall bruise you on the head, and you shall bruise him on the heel."

    d. "But He was pierced through for our transgressions, He was crushed for our iniquities; the chastening for our well-being fell upon Him, and by His scourging we are healed."

15. A high official under Kings Nebuchadnezzar, Belshazzar, and Darius was the prophet

    a. Ezekiel.
    b. Daniel.
    c. Isaiah.
    d. Jeremiah.

16. Most of the prophetical books were written during the time covered by the historical book of

    a. Judges.
    b. 2 Samuel.
    c. Ezra.
    d. 2 Kings.

17. The prophet who wept over the destruction of Jerusalem and the sin which prompted it was

    a. Isaiah.
    b. Jeremiah.
    c. Ezekiel.
    d. Daniel.

18. A covenant was a(n)

   a. order issued by a ruler.
   b. curse.
   c. agreement or contract.
   d. oath.

19. The prophet who envisioned the glory of God, the sinfulness of Jerusalem, and a magnificent, restored temple was

   a. Isaiah.
   b. Ezekiel.
   c. Daniel.
   d. Jeremiah.

20. "For a child will be born to us, a son will be given to us; and the government will rest on His shoulders; and His name will be called Wonderful Counselor, Mighty God, Eternal Father, Prince of Peace."

   The prophet who described the first and second coming of the Messiah in the above verse was

   a. Zechariah.
   b. Daniel.
   c. Isaiah.
   d. none of the above.

21. The first to identify himself by the term *prophet* was

   a. Moses.
   b. Samuel.
   c. David.
   d. Abraham.

22. The percentage of Scripture that could be considered prophetic when it was written was approximately

   a. 1 percent.
   b. 10 percent.
   c. 25 percent.
   d. 75 percent.

23. The minor prophet who recorded the most messianic prophecies was

   a. Malachi.
   b. Zechariah.
   c. Haggai.
   d. Joel.

24. The woman listed below who was *not* called a prophetess
   was

   a. Isaiah's wife.
   b. Abigail.
   c. Deborah.
   d. Miriam.

25. The significant event dated by Daniel's "sixty-nine weeks" is

   a. the Crucifixion.
   b. the fall of Babylon.
   c. the end of the Noahic covenant.
   d. the birth of Christ.

26. The two prophets who preached primarily to the Northern
   Kingdom were

   a. Ezekiel and Daniel.
   b. Haggai and Zechariah.
   c. Amos and Hosea.
   d. none of the above.

27. In Micah, Israel and Judah are hauled into court. Micah's
   charges and God's testimony indicate that the people are
   guilty of violating the

   a. Abrahamic covenant.
   b. Noahic covenant.
   c. Davidic covenant.
   d. Mosaic covenant.

28. Reflecting Israel's unfaithfulness toward God is the marriage of Gomer and

    a. Malachi.
    b. Hosea.
    c. Nahum.
    d. Ezekiel.

29. The sin that Malachi did *not* charge against Israel was

    a. divorce.
    b. warring against Edom, their kinsmen.
    c. ungodly priests and leaders.
    d. withholding tithes.

30. The following verse *not* found in Micah is:

    a. "In the year of King Uzziah's death, I saw the Lord sitting on a throne, lofty and exalted, with the train of His robe filling the temple."

    b. "Then they will hammer their swords into plowshares and their spears into pruning hooks; nation will not lift up sword against nation, and never again will they train for war."

    c. "He has told you, O man, what is good; and what does the Lord require of you but to do justice, to love kindness, and to walk humbly with your God?"

    d. "But as for you, Bethlehem Ephrathah, too little to be among the clans of Judah, from you One will go forth for Me to be ruler in Israel."

31. During the Return, the prophet(s) who urged the rebuilding of the temple was/were

    a. Haggai and Zechariah.
    b. Malachi.
    c. Ezekiel and Daniel.
    d. Obadiah.

32. In the prophetical books, "the remnant of Israel" referred
    to

    a. the poor and needy.
    b. schools of prophets.
    c. a small number of Jacob's descendants through whom
       God worked at pivotal times.
    d. the aliens who lived in Israel during the Exile.

33. The "new covenant" expanded the older

    a. Abrahamic covenant.
    b. Noahic covenant.
    c. Edenic covenant.
    d. Mosaic covenant.

34. Jesus compared Himself to the prophet

    a. Jeremiah.
    b. Joel.
    c. Jonah.
    d. Elisha.

35. Over ninety times God addressed as "son of man" the
    prophet

    a. Jeremiah.
    b. Daniel.
    c. Isaiah.
    d. Ezekiel.

36. Bringing God's response when Hezekiah prayed, "Incline
    Thine ear, O Lord, and hear; open Thine eyes, O Lord,
    and see; and listen to all the words of Sennacherib" was the
    prophet

    a. Isaiah.
    b. Daniel.
    c. Ezekiel.
    d. Jeremiah.

37. The prophet who used locusts to picture the devastation of God's judgment on an unrepentant nation was

    a. Hosea.
    b. Amos.
    c. Haggai.
    d. Joel.

38. The subject of Isaiah 53 is

    a. the seraphims' adoration of God.
    b. the fall of Lucifer.
    c. the Suffering Servant.
    d. the prophecy of Cyrus.

39. Micaiah, Nathan, Elijah, and Elisha were all prophets. They also had in common the fact that

    a. all were murdered.
    b. none were Jews.
    c. all prophesied under King David.
    d. none left written records that survived.

40. "And it is He [God] who changes the times and the epochs; He removes kings and establishes kings . . . "
    The above passage is a prayer of

    a. Isaiah.
    b. Daniel.
    c. Jonah.
    d. Habakkuk.

41. The prophet who used a valley of dry bones to describe Israel's future was

    a. Ezekiel.
    b. Daniel.
    c. Isaiah.
    d. Jeremiah.

42. God's attitude toward diviners and spiritists was

    a. He made no comment about them.

b. He detested them.

c. He praised their skill.

d. He provided cities of refuge for them.

43. The prophet who focused his short book on the judgment of Edom was

a. Obadiah.

b. Jonah.

c. Habakkuk.

d. Malachi.

44. There was no king in Jerusalem after the Exile because

a. the line of David had been destroyed.

b. Israel was still under Gentile rule.

c. the Jews and the Samaritans could not agree about a king.

d. there weren't enough tribes registered to elect a king.

45. "And it shall be in the last days," God says, "that I will pour forth of My Spirit upon all mankind; and your sons and your daughters shall prophesy, and your young men shall see visions, and your old men shall dream dreams . . . "

In the preceding passage (Acts 2:17), Peter was recalling the prophetic words of

a. Isaiah.

b. Daniel.

c. Hosea.

d. Joel.

46. Daniel anticipates the time when God will establish an everlasting kingdom. The covenant that promised the kingdom was the

a. Abrahamic.

b. Mosaic.

c. Noahic.

d. Davidic.

47. A seer was

    a. a sorcerer.
    b. a prophet.
    c. a potter.
    d. a seamstress.

48. The prophet who envisioned a plumb line and a basketful of summer fruit as he sought Israel's repentance was

    a. Amos.
    b. Joel.
    c. Daniel.
    d. Ezekiel.

49. The one *not* called a prophet in the New Testament was

    a. Simeon.
    b. Zacharias.
    c. John the Baptist.
    d. Luke.

50. "Behold, I am going to send you Elijah the prophet before the coming of the great and terrible day of the Lord. And he will restore the hearts of the fathers to their children, and the hearts of the children to their fathers, lest I come and smite the land with a curse." The preceding passage ends the prophetical book of

    a. Jeremiah.
    b. Habakkuk.
    c. Malachi.
    d. Daniel.

Answers

1. (d.) The prophets were not self-motivated; they were "men moved by the Holy Spirit" (2 Peter 1:21). Their authority, appointment, and communication came from God. In a modern sense, the prophets were God's "administrative assistants." Amos 3:7 called them servants:

> Surely the Lord God does nothing
> Unless He reveals His secret counsel
> to His servants the prophets.

The prophets spoke to individuals, to the tribes, and occasionally to Israel's neighbors, heralding their messages with the special phrase, "Thus says the Lord."

2. (b.) Isaiah's words of comfort signal the shift between the twin themes characteristic of all prophetical writings: judgment and hope (or condemnation and consolation). With one exception (see answer 50), the prophetical books begin with judgment and end with hope.

Isaiah's sixty-six books are unique because they seem to parallel the Bible as a whole. The first thirty-nine chapters, like the Old Testament, highlight God's holiness and man's sinfulness. Isaiah's last twenty-seven chapters, like the New Testament, describe God's provision for man's sinful state. Isaiah is the most quoted prophet in the New Testament.

3. (c.) The office of a prophet did not entail temple duties unless the prophet was also a priest. Only three men played this dual role: Jeremiah, Ezekiel, and Zechariah. In addition to exposing sin, warning of God's judgment, and proclaiming Messiah's coming, the prophets appealed for personal purity, urged social and civil reforms, and prayed.

4. (a.) Jonah's distaste for his Assyrian assignment reflected Israel's wary attitude toward Gentiles. The Assyrians were not lovable; they were notoriously cruel. Jonah's mission was equivalent to Bob Hope's preaching U.S. patriotism to the Ayatollah Khomeini. So, the prophet's angry pout at the Ninevehites' repentance is perhaps more understandable than his reaction to the "death" of his little shady vine. In Jonah, God's mind is on the lost; the prophet's is on his own comfort.

5. (b.) The length of a prophet's message dictated whether he was labeled "major" or "minor."

6. (d.) Joel and Zephaniah emphasized the "day of the Lord." This widely used prophetic expression (mentioned also in Isaiah, Jeremiah, Ezekiel, Amos, Obadiah, Zechariah, and Malachi) was associated with judgment on Israel (Joel 1:15; Amos 5:18, 20; Zephaniah 1:4–13) and on her enemies (Joel

3:1–17; Zephaniah 2:4–15), or with a time of universal judgment (Zephaniah 1:18; 3:8). It also referred to a period of intense suffering and purification (Zephaniah 1:15; 3:13).

7. (c.) The true test of a prophet was the accuracy of his
predictions (Deuteronomy 18:20–22). The Israelites had long
been exposed to the Egyptians who "divined" the future. The
Canaanites in the Promised Land perpetuated the practice.
Therefore, God provided the accuracy test (100 percent) as a
sign that the prophet was authorized to reveal the future.

8. (a.) Nahum preached the message bubbling from the
heart of Jonah: destruction to the Ninevehites. Nahum, God's
back-up prophet to the Assyrians, returned to Nineveh about
one hundred years after Jonah's "great revival." Nahum's message would have warmed Jonah's heart and pleased the Southern Kingdom of Judah as well, since Judah had already seen
the Assyrians swallow up the Northern Kingdom.

9. (a.) Zephaniah was a minor prophet. Jeremiah, Isaiah,
Daniel, and Ezekiel make up the major prophet quartet.

10. (c.) Habakkuk detested the widespread sin in Judah, but
he was horrified when he learned that the nation chosen to
chastise God's people was Babylon, the "dreaded and feared," a
nation whose "justice and authority originated with themselves." In his dismay, Habakkuk cried out to God who reminded the prophet: "the righteous will live by his faith" (Habakkuk 2:4). Encouraged, Habakkuk responded: "Though the
fig tree should not blossom . . . " (3:17–18).

11. (d.) Daniel's prophecy was a good news/bad news message. The good news was that Israel would go home from Babylon, but the bad news was that the Gentiles would continue to
rule. Daniel's interpretation of the metal and clay image described the succession of dominating world empires (Daniel
2:31–49). His explanation was expanded in chapter 7 with the
vision of the four creatures. Luke described this period of Gentile dominance as "the times of the Gentiles" (Luke 21:20–28).

12. (a.) When we think of a prophet, we usually think about
predicting the future or "foretelling," the more spectacular side
of the ministry. In reality, a prophet spent most of his life as a
forthteller, one who proclaimed God's word to the people. The
prophet was part historian, part newscaster, part instructor,

part motivator, and part disciplinarian. Prophets at times were also called upon to act out "object lessons" for the nation (Isaiah 8:3–4; Ezekiel 14:1–8).

13. (d.) Jeremiah wrote: "And this whole land shall be a desolation and a horror, and these nations shall serve the king of Babylon seventy years" (Jeremiah 25:11–14; 29:10).

While his prediction was probably not encouraging to the exiles who had just trekked into captivity, some six decades later, the statement overwhelmed Daniel, who grasped its significance and interceded for his nation (Daniel 9:2–19).

Jeremiah, a priest in Jerusalem, became a prophet during godly King Josiah's reign (627 B.C.) After Josiah's death, sin permeated every echelon of life. Jeremiah prophesied for forty years, using objects—a ruined linen sash, wine jugs, drought, a potter and his clay—to teach spiritual lessons. In spite of the lessons, Judah plunged deeper into apostasy.

Jeremiah is often called the "weeping prophet." He had a lot to weep about! The people and priests ignored or ridiculed his messages. He was imprisoned, beaten, dumped in a cistern, and kidnapped. He lived to see his prophecies about the destruction of Jerusalem come true. Jeremiah's contemporaries were Habakkuk and Zephaniah.

14. (c.) In Eden, God provided assurance to the fallen couple that the Messiah, the seed of the woman, would crushed the head of Satan.

15. (b.) Daniel hobnobbed with the "rich and famous" and often predicted their royal misfortunes. Because of his government position and comfortable surroundings, Daniel is seldom associated with suffering. Yet adversity was no stranger to him. Throughout his life Daniel obeyed his soveriegn Lord, whom he called the "Ancient of Days" (Daniel 7:9,13). It is ironic that Daniel, who remembered his homeland so fondly and who encouraged others so faithfully, never saw Jerusalem again.

16. (d.) Most of the prophetical books parallel the period of 2 Kings. The exceptions were Daniel and Ezekiel, who prophesied during the Exile, and Haggai, Zechariah, and Malachi, who wrote during the Return. There were active prophets at others times, but the majority of written prophecies were recorded during the later kingdom period.

17. (b.) In Lamentations Jeremiah saw the "curses" of Deuteronomy 28 played out in the streets of Jerusalem. His lament, a poem written to express personal sorrow, reviewed Israel's sinful history. Rather than wallowing in grief, however, Jeremiah trusted God to keep His covenant and to restore the nation.

18. (c.) A covenant was a legal agreement between two parties. Biblical covenants fell into two categories: unilateral (unconditional) where God was responsible for keeping the covenant, and bilateral (conditional) where God and man both had responsibilities. The sins which the Old Testament prophets brought to Israel's attention were actually covenantal infringements.

19. (b.) Ezekiel was the visionary. Although some of his visions leave the reader a little dizzy, it is helpful to remember that Ezekiel received two commissions. During his first commission, he preached judgment and saw the glory of God (chapter 1) and the sinfulness of Jerusalem (chapters 8–11). During his second commission, after Jerusalem fell, Ezekiel proclaimed restoration. The prophet saw the vision of the dry bones (chapter 37) and the magnificent millennial temple (chapters 40–47).

20. (c.) Isaiah recorded the most messianic prophecies. In Isaiah 9:6, the prophet magnificently highlighted the Messiah's birth and four of His future roles: Wonderful Counselor, Mighty God, Eternal Father, and Prince of Peace.

21. (a.) In the Pentateuch Moses wrote: "The Lord your God will raise up for you a prophet like me from among you, from your countrymen, you shall listen to Him" (Deuteronomy 18:15). The verse also foretold of Jesus' role as prophet.

22. (c.) Approximately 25 percent of Scripture was prophetic when written. In the Old Testament alone there are 1,527 verses about the second coming of Christ, a future event.

23. (b.) Zechariah is second to Isaiah in recording messianic prophecies. In one night Zechariah had eight visions, where he saw both the first and second Comings of Jesus (Zechariah 3:8; 6:12). Most of Zechariah's messianic prophecies are described in two oracles found in chapters 9–14. Because Zechariah's book contains fourteen chapters, he is often called the "major" of the minor prophets.

24. (b.) Abigail, one of David's wives, was not a prophetess. Isaiah's wife (Isaiah 8:3), Deborah (Judges 4:4–9), and Miriam (Exodus 15:20) were given the title.

25. (a.) The message Gabriel passed on to Daniel pinpointed the end of the "sixty-ninth week" as the time at which the Messiah would be "cut off" (killed) in Jerusalem. Hence, the date of the Crucifixion was fixed at 483 years after the decree to rebuild Jerusalem (Daniel 9:24–27; Nehemiah 2:1–8).

26. (c.) Amos and Hosea prophesied to the Northern Kingdom. Amos predated Hosea, but both preached judgment to a nation wallowing in affluence.

27. (d.) Sin, called out in any prophetical book, represented a breach of the Mosaic Covenant. This covenant, instituted in Exodus 19, renewed in Exodus 34:10–32, and ratified in Deuteronomy 26:16–19, was the only bilateral covenant that God made with the nation. The Abrahamic, Davidic, and Noahic covenants were unilateral covenants for which God was solely responsible, and the fulfillment of these covenants was not dependent upon the performance of the people.

28. (b.) Hosea's entire family, including his wife Gomer, was an ominous sign to Israel. God pronounced judgment as He named Hosea's children. With the first son, God announced: "Name him Jezreel; for yet a little while, and I will punish the house of Jehu for the bloodshed of Jezreel, and I will put an end to the kingdom of the house of Israel" (1:4). Hosea's second child brought greater judgment: "Name her Lo-ruhamah, for I will no longer have compassion on the house of Israel, that I should ever forgive them" (1:6). The last child brought separation: "Name him Lo-ammi, for you are not My people and I am not your God" (1:9).

29. (b.) Israel had not attacked Edom. In Malachi's day the nation backslid into old sinful habits of corrupt leadership, ritualistic worship, and ungodly marital relationships.

30. (a.) In the year King Uzziah died, Isaiah, not Micah, saw the Lord (Isaiah 6:1–13). The swords and spears are found in Micah 4:3; the requirements of the Lord in Micah 6:8; and the birthplace of the Messiah is identified in Micah 5:2.

31. (a.) Haggai and Zechariah urged the rebuilding of the temple, the foundation of which had been laid in 536 B.C. Be-

tween 535–520 construction stopped. In 520, Haggai urged the people to complete the work and a few months later Zechariah joined him. The prophets attributed the temple's disrepair to spiritual apathy. However, Ezra 4 suggests that outside forces also contributed to the delay.

32. (c.) The remnant was a small number of Jacob's descendants through whom God worked. The remnant was not a "shielded" group of people, they were survivors: "For out of Jerusalem shall go forth a remnant, and out of Mount Zion survivors" (Isaiah 37:32). Isaiah, Jeremiah, Ezekiel and seven of the minor prophets mentioned the remnant.

33. (d.) The new covenant, outlined in Jeremiah 31, expanded the Mosaic covenant. As a ministry of the Holy Spirit (Ezekiel 36:24–32), God's law would be written on people's hearts not on stone tablets (31:33). Sin was forgiven (31:34) because the penalty was paid (Isaiah 53:4–6). In addition, Israel regained a national identity (Jeremiah 31:35–36). The new covenant included the Northern and Southern kingdoms, even though both still suffered from their infringements of the Mosaic covenant (Jeremiah 31:31). The fulfillment of the new covenant for Israel remains a future event.

34. (c.) Jesus said, "for just as Jonah was three days and three nights in the belly of the sea monster, so shall the Son of Man be three days and three nights in the heart of the earth" (Matthew 12:40; Luke 11:30).

35. (d.) Beginning with the prophet's first commissioning service (Ezekiel 2:1) and continuing through his temple vision (47:6), God addressed Ezekiel as "son of man," a phrase which stressed Ezekiel's association with humanity.

36. (a.) A prophet's ministry was not usually filled with high, spiritual moments. Isaiah, who had prophesied during the reign of Ahaz (one of Judah's worst kings), must have been encouraged when Hezekiah looked to God for a solution to Sennacherib (Isaiah 36–37). If Isaiah outlived Hezekiah and prophesied during the rule of the vile King Manasseh, this incident may have been one of his last high moments.

37. (d.) Joel's locust plague was an actual natural disaster. It could be likened to the assassination of John F. Kennedy, an event so singular it became a byword among the generations.

The devastation set the stage for Joel's prophecy which described "the day of the Lord."

38. (c.) Isaiah 53 details God's "suffering servant," prophetically previewing Christ's earthly ministry.

39. (d.) The men are "oral" prophets who left no written records of their ministries.

40. (b.) Daniel, one of the Bible's great pray-ers, understood that God bestowed or withdrew power according to His purpose (Daniel 2:21). It a fact well worth remembering in any age.

41. (a.) Ezekiel's wrote to the discouraged exiles. His vision of the Valley of Dry Bones (and the re-united sticks) in chapter 37 reinforced God's promises of restoration and reunification outlined in chapter 36.

42. (b.) God detested diviners, mediums, and spiritists (Leviticus 19:31; 20:27; Deuteronomy 18:10–12; 20–22; 2 Kings 17:17). God wanted Israel to look to Him for hope for the future: "And when they say to you, 'Consult the mediums and the spiritists who whisper and mutter,' should not a people consult their God?" (Isaiah 8:19).

43. (a.) Two themes stand out in Obadiah: God defends His people and pride goes before destruction. The Edomites were kinsmen of the Israelites through Esau. Because of their wealth, mining industry, and almost impregnable capital city of Petra, the arrogant Edomites believed they were invincible. When Jerusalem was attacked, the Edomites cheered, looted the city, killed the fleeing inhabitants, and handed the survivors over to the enemy (Obadiah 12–14). God remembered and judged their deeds.

44. (b.) When the Exile ended, Israel was under Gentile rule. Hosea had anticipated the situation: "For the sons of Israel will remain for many days without king or prince. . . . Afterward the sons of Israel will return and seek the Lord their God and David their king; and they will come trembling to the Lord and to His goodness in the last days" (Hosea 3:4–5). Both Haggai (1:1) and Zechariah (1:1), postexilic prophets, reference time by Darius, a Gentile king.

45. (d.) Joel received a lot of attention in the New Testament. In the Olivet Discourse (Matthew 24:29), Jesus tied the events of His second coming to Joel 2:10, 31 and 3:15. At Pen-

tecost (Acts 2:17–21), Peter quoted from Joel (2:28–32a). In Romans 10:13 Paul mentioned Joel (2:32) in connection with Gentile salvation.

46. (d.) The "everlasting kingdom" mentioned in Daniel 7:14 was promised under the Davidic covenant (2 Samuel 7:16).

47. (b.) According to 1 Samuel 9:9, a seer was another name for a prophet: "(Formerly in Israel, when a man went to inquire of God, he used to say, 'Come, and let us go to the seer'; for he who is called a prophet now was formerly called a seer.)" The word was used in Chronicles, Isaiah, and Micah.

48. (a.) Amos was the forerunner of the home missionary. He was born in the Southern Kingdom but sent to prophesy in the Northern Kingdom. Amos was a farmer, a herdsman, a grower of sycamore figs, hardly the perfect person to relate to the problems of affluent Israel. Yet, Amos' no nonsense, farm-oriented language was exactly what the sophisticated, economically secure Israelites needed. Amos called the wealthy, pampered women "cows of Bashan" (4:1) and referred to the greedy businessmen as "you who trample the needy" (8:4). Amos was a direct, hard-hitting prophet.

49. (d.) Luke, the Gentile physician, was not a prophet, but he wrote about three men, beside Jesus, who were: Simeon (Luke 2:25–35), Zacharias (1:67–69), and John the Baptist (1:57–80). While the prophetic office did not disappear in the New Testament, many of the prophet's duties were transferred to the apostles and other leaders who became "foretellers" and "forthtellers" to the church.

50. (c.) Malachi, the only prophetical book which does not end on hope, concludes by peering at the "great and terrible day of the Lord."

HISTORY: NEW TESTAMENT

ONCE UPON A TIME, A SMALL, HUNGRY DOG stole a piece of meat from an unsuspecting butcher. The angry shopkeeper raced after the thief, but it wasn't long before the dog, the superior runner, was settling along the river's bank to enjoy his midday snack.

Imagine the mutt's surprise when he glanced into the water and saw, just inches away, another dog with a bigger piece of meat than his own! Instantly, the greedy hound reached for the meat, dropped his chop in the water, and was left with nothing at all to eat.

Moral: In reaching for the shadow we may lose the substance.

The pup from Aesop's *Fables* isn't the only part of creation having a hard time with substance and shadow. The same human imagination that permitted Adam to name the animals has made it difficult for the fallen sons of Adam to distinguish between the truth of substance and the lure of shadow.

In the Old Testament, God presented Israel with substance, a plan of redemption for mankind through a promised Messiah. The promise was wrapped in words and it was hard for the nation to hold onto the words. In bad times, Israel cried out, and the promise seemed real. In good times, the promise blurred and Israel chased the shadowy gods of neighboring tribes.

In the New Testament God's Word was made flesh; the Messiah became substance. They called Him Jesus, and God approved Him by miracles and signs and fulfilled prophecies. But men still had a hard time distinguishing substance from shadow. The miracles and signs were greeted by a clamor for more miracles and more signs. The prophecies were ignored or dismissed.

Jesus presented Himself as the substance of eternal life, yet His audience clung to a shadowy earthly kingdom. Jesus offered the substance of grace, but the Jews chose the shadow of the law. Jesus presented the reality of servanthood, but His disciples sought the elusiveness of rank.

The New Testament offers a clear choice. From the opening genealogy of Matthew to the closing benediction of Revelation, the reader is reminded of the contrast between substance, God's righteous standards, and shadow, man's impulsive imaginings. Each aspect of Christ's life—His teachings, His activities, His church, and His new covenant—reinforces God's redemptive plan in such a direct way that Pilate's question "What shall I do with Jesus?" becomes the question of the ages.

What will *I* do with Jesus? What will *you* do with Jesus? Before any of us can decide what to do with Jesus, we must know Who He is.

Introducing Jesus is the task of the "histories" of the New Testament, the four Gospels and the book of Acts. These historical books tie together three distinct spiritual threads: the gospel of Jesus Christ, the establishment of His church, and the extension of the "good news" to the Gentiles through missions.

Like the opening of a tightly closed rosebud, the final revelation of God's redemptive plan for man unfolds in the Gospels and Acts. Yet, the thrust of the New Testament is not history, but belief. Ultimately, each of us must choose whether Jesus Christ is substance or shadow.

Questions

1. Jesus chose _____ men to be His Apostles.
   a. seventy

b. twelve

c. seven

d. four

2. The Jewish feast coinciding with the birth of the church was

a. Pentecost.

b. Purim.

c. Passover.

d. Jubilee.

3. Jesus' birth was unique because His mother was

a. very old.

b. a virgin.

c. a descendant of Aaron.

d. a prophetess.

4. Appearing on the Mount of Transfiguration with Jesus were

a. Enoch and Elijah.

b. Elijah and Moses.

c. Moses and David.

d. David and John the Baptist.

5. The disciple who helped an Ethiopian eunuch understand Isaiah's prophecy was

a. Peter.

b. Paul.

c. Philip.

d. Stephen.

6. A detailed account of Jesus' early ministry, His first miracle, and His encounter with the woman at the well were given by

a. Matthew.

b. Mark.

c. Luke.

d. John.

7. Jesus first appeared after His resurrection to

   a. the apostles.
   b. Mary Magdalene.
   c. Peter.
   d. Roman soldiers.

8. Peter was led to begin preaching to the Gentiles by the prayers of

   a. Simon the tanner.
   b. Paul.
   c. Dorcas.
   d. Cornelius.

9. Jesus taught the Pharisees that the whole law and the prophets rested on two commandments. One commandment was: "You shall love the Lord your God with all your heart, and with all your soul, and with all your mind." The other commandment was

   a. "Honor thy father and thy mother."
   b. "Remember the Sabbath."
   c. "You shall not steal."
   d. "Love your neighbor as yourself."

10. Jesus made several converts during the early days of His ministry among the unlikely group of

    a. Roman soldiers.
    b. Samaritans.
    c. men of Nazareth.
    d. Pharisees and scribes.

11. The first Christian martyr was

    a. Ananias.
    b. Paul.
    c. Stephen.
    d. Matthias.

12. Jesus was in Bethlehem

    a. at His birth.
    b. at age twelve, when he talked with the temple teachers.
    c. at His baptism.
    d. all of the above tims.

13. "Thou are the Christ, the Son of the living God" was said by

    a. Peter.
    b. John.
    c. Thomas.
    d. none of the above.

14. On his third missionary journey, after Paul was imprisoned in Palestine,

    a. he was crucified.
    b. he was set free.
    c. he was sent to Rome.
    d. he was killed by a mob.

15. "An evil and adulterous generation craves for a sign; and yet no sign shall be given to it but the sign of _____ the prophet."

    a. Jonah
    b. Moses
    c. Elijah
    d. Isaiah

16. Jesus washed the feet of His disciples

    a. at the wedding feast in Cana.
    b. when He prepared breakfast by the Sea of Galilee.
    c. when He dined with Martha and Mary.
    d. when He hosted their last Passover meal together.

17. Paul's sermon on Mars Hill in Athens was prompted by

    a. idols.
    b. an earthquake.

c. the seven sons of Sceva.

d. temple prostitution.

18. The Jews wanted to kill Jesus because

   a. He broke the Sabbath.
   b. He called God His "Father."
   c. He made Himself equal with God.
   d. all of the above.

19. Jesus' first recorded miracle was

   a. calming the turbulent sea.
   b. feeding the five thousand.
   c. changing water into wine.
   d. restoring a severed ear.

20. During his three missionary journeys Paul did *not* visit

   a. Galatia.
   b. Greece.
   c. Asia Minor.
   d. Egypt and North Africa.

21. "Hosanna! Blessed is He Who comes in the Name of the Lord; blessed is the coming kingdom of our father David; hosanna in the highest!"

   Jesus was welcomed with the preceding greeting at

   a. His dedication in the temple.
   b. His birth.
   c. His triumphal entry into Jerusalem.
   d. His resurrection.

22. Jesus was identified as both "the Lamb of God" and "the Son of God" by

   a. John the Baptist.
   b. the men of Nazareth.
   c. Nicodemus.
   d. the Magi.

23. The acknowledged leader of the early church was

    a. John.
    b. Gamaliel.
    c. Paul.
    d. Peter.

24. Responding to each of Satan's recorded temptations in the desert, Jesus

    a. ignored Satan.
    b. called legions of angels.
    c. said, "Get behind Me, Satan! You are a stumbling block to Me."
    d. quoted Scripture.

25. The subject of the "Olivet Discourse" was

    a. the Good Shepherd.
    b. end time signs and events.
    c. the role of the church.
    d. stewardship.

26. Paul was attacked in Jerusalem after he returned from his third missionary journey by

    a. Roman soldiers.
    b. money-changers.
    c. the Jews.
    d. the Greeks.

27. The verse that is *not* a part of the Sermon on the Mount is:

    a. "You are the light of the world. A city set on a hill cannot be hidden."

    b. "Greater love has no one than this, that one lay down his life for his friends."

    c. "Our Father who art in heaven, Hallowed be Thy name."

d. "Not everyone who says to me, 'Lord, Lord,' will enter the kingdom of heaven; but he who does the will of My Father who is in heaven."

28. Jesus was crucified on the authority of

a. Herod.
b. Caiaphas.
c. the Sanhedrin.
d. Pilate.

29. Commissioned with Paul for the first missionary journey was

a. Barnabas.
b. Philip.
c. Timothy.
d. James, the half brother of Jesus.

30. The proof that validated Jesus' baptism was

a. the waters of the Jordan parted.
b. a voice from heaven affirmed Him.
c. Elijah appeared.
d. Jesus immediately healed a blind man.

31. The parable *not* used to teach about the kingdom of heaven was

a. the rich man and Lazarus.
b. tares among the wheat.
c. a pearl of great price.
d. a grown mustard seed.

32. The birthplace of the church occurred at

a. Capernaum.
b. Bethany.
c. Jerusalem.
d. none of the above.

33. When Jesus began His public ministry, He cleansed the temple at Passover. Afterward, the man who came to see Him by night was

    a. John the Baptist.
    b. Nicodemus.
    c. Zacchaeus.
    d. Matthew.

34. Saul's conversion came as a direct result of

    a. a heavenly vision.
    b. the faith of the Christians in Damascus.
    c. Philip's preaching.
    d. Stephen's trial.

35. Early in Jesus' ministry, He "introduced" Himself as the Messiah and

    a. became a well-respected temple leader.
    b. called men to His church.
    c. challenged the authority of Rome over the Jews.
    d. challenged the people to repent and live righteously.

36. Judas hanged himself

    a. the day of the Crucifixion.
    b. the day after the Crucifixion.
    c. the morning of the Resurrection.
    d. the day before the Crucifixion.

37. The group of elders from whom Paul took his leave by reviewing his ministry to them, sharing his concerns, and reminding them of their leadership responsibilities were at

    a. Antioch.
    b. Jerusalem.
    c. Ephesus.
    d. None of the above.

38. Besides the miracles, Jesus' authority was borne witness by

    a. the traditions of the Pharisees.

b. the Scriptures.

c. the crowds who followed.

d. Pilate's tolerance toward Jesus.

39. Jesus cleansed the temple for the last time

a. just before He raised Lazarus.

b. after the Last Supper.

c. after His triumphal entry into Jerusalem.

d. none of the above.

40. The event that did *not* occur during Paul's missionary journey was

a. Paul's assuring 276 sailing mates of their safety.

b. Paul's befriending Timothy.

c. a jailer's conversion.

d. Paul's instructions to the church at Corinth.

41. Gethsemane was

a. unleavened bread.

b. an olive grove.

c. a place of execution.

d. the city where Lazarus lived.

42. The disciples questioned whether Jesus should go to the "ailing" Lazarus because

a. there was a famine in Judea.

b. Rome was persecuting the Jews around Jerusalem.

c. the Jews had previously tried to stone Jesus.

d. Jesus would have to pass through Samaria.

43. Felix and Festus were

a. early converts of Paul.

b. Roman officials during Paul's imprisonment.

c. elders of the church at Jerusalem.

d. Jewish religious leaders during Paul's imprisonment.

44. As the religious leaders opposed Jesus more openly, His response was that

    a. Jesus warned the Pharisees and scribes about their attitudes.
    b. Jesus intensified the disciples' training.
    c. Jesus stressed the cost of discipleship.
    d. all of the above.

45. *After* Stephen's trial,

    a. the Jews made peace with the church.
    b. Paul began the first missionary journey.
    c. the Jews persecuted the church.
    d. Rome persecuted the church.

46. According to Matthew, Mark, and Luke, Jesus died around the ninth hour, the present-day time of

    a. 9:00 A.M.
    b. noon.
    c. 3:00 P.M.
    d. 6:00 P.M.

47. The decision of the church council at Jerusalem concerning the Gentiles was that

    a. the Gentiles had to be circumcised.
    b. the Gentiles did not have to be circumcised.
    c. only the apostles could preach to the Gentiles.
    d. none of the above.

48. According to genealogy, Jesus was a son of the tribe of

    a. Benjamin.
    b. Levi.
    c. Judah.
    d. none of the above.

49. The result of the apostles' statement, "It is not desirable for us to neglect the word of God in order to serve tables," was that

   a. the church stopped providing food.
   b. deacons were selected.
   c. apostles dealt with food only after they had seen to prayer and the ministry of the Word.
   d. Ananias and Sapphira were chosen to serve tables.

50. John the Baptist was

   a. Jesus' kinsman.
   b. the "friend of the bridegroom."
   c. the prophet who baptized Jesus.
   d. all of the above.

Answers

1. (b.) In His early ministry, Jesus had many followers. The selection of the apostles, however, came during His Galilean ministry, not at the beginning of His public life. Jesus had been baptized, interviewed Nicodemus, moved his headquarters to Capernaum, and performed several miracles before the apostles were given their official title. Jesus chose the apostles after a night of prayer (Luke 6:12).

2. (a.) "And when the day of Pentecost had come, they were all together in one place" (Acts 2:1). It is significant that the church was born on Pentecost, because Pentecost was one of the three great feast days in the life of a Jew. Jewish men from all parts of the world were in Jerusalem to celebrate. It was to these devout men "from every nation under heaven" (Acts 2:5) that the Spirit-empowered disciples began to share the gospel, and each visitor understood in his native language. Many of these new converts (Hellenists) became part of the Jerusalem church.

3. (b.) Dr. Luke noted that an astonished Mary acknowledged her virginity before Gabriel: "How can this be, since I am a virgin?" (Luke 1:34). Isaiah, of course, had predicted Jesus' virgin birth 650 years earlier (Isaiah 7:14). Isaiah's

prophecy was used to convince Joseph, Mary's fiance, that the expected child was indeed the legitimate Son of God.

4. (b.) Matthew (17:1–8), Mark (9:2–13), and Luke (9:28–36) record the Transfiguration event. Each writer clearly lists the "visitors" as Elijah and Moses. Since only three apostles witnessed the event, the identification came from Peter, James, or John after the Resurrection.

5. (c.) The Philip who taught the eunuch was not the Galilean apostle, but a man from Caesarea who came to prominence in Acts as a deacon in the early church. Philip was a fearless, Spirit-led evangelist who preached his way through Judea and Samaria after Stephen's death (Acts 8). Philip sheltered Paul on his last journey to Jerusalem (Acts 21:8–10).

6. (d.) John records the miracle at Cana, Jesus' first cleansing of the temple, his interview with Nicodemus, and the encounter with the Samaritan woman (John 1–4).

7. (b.) There was much confusion the morning the Lord arose from the dead, but according to Mark 16:19, Jesus first appeared to Mary Magdalene. John 20:18 verifies the appearance.

8. (d.) Cornelius, the Roman centurion who lived in Caesarea (and may have heard Philip preach), was "one who feared God . . . and prayed to God continually" (Acts10:2). As a direct result of Cornelius' prayers, Peter preached the gospel to this Roman officer, and thereby opened the doors of Christianity to the Gentiles (Acts 10:22–48).

9. (d.) For an unnamed Pharisaic lawyer—one accustomed to legal hair-splitting—Jesus reduced all spiritual concerns to two basic commandments (Matthew 22:36–40). The lawyer had no rebuttal!

10. (b.) Jesus made a number of converts among the Samaritans, the enemies of the Jews (John 4:39–43). Overall, He was better received in Samaria than in His own home town.

11. (c.) Stephen was one of the deacons in the Jerusalem church. His faith was soon tried by the Sanhedrin, the "Supreme Court" of the Jews. Acts 7 records Stephen's eloquent defense which precipitated a violent response. Stephen, charged with blasphemy, was dragged out of the city and stoned (Acts 7:54–60). Paul (than Saul) assented to the verdict.

12. (a.) Jesus was born in Bethlehem during the reign of the Roman Emperor, Caesar Augustus (Luke 2:1–7). Shortly before Jesus' birth, Caesar had ordered a census, and all Jews were required to return to the city of their fathers to register. Although pregnant women did not customarily make long trips (seventy miles from Nazareth to Bethlehem), both Mary and Joseph knew that the Messiah was to be born in Bethlehem, as Micah had prophesied (5:2). After a six-week stay in Bethlehem, Mary and Joseph went to Jerusalem to perform the purification rites prescribed in Leviticus 12:1–8 (Luke 2:21–24, 39). There is no mention in Scripture that Jesus ever returned to the place of His birth.

13. (a.) Peter's remarkable statement precipitated a change in Christ's relationship with His apostles. From then on, Jesus emphasized His death, the cost of discipleship, and the disciples' leadership responsibilities (Matthew 16:13–20:24).

14. (c.) Even though several authorities—some Pharisees (Acts 23:9), Claudius Lysias (Acts 23:26–29), Festus (Acts 25:24–25), and Agrippa (Acts 26:32)—pronounced Paul "innocent," he was sent to Rome as a prisoner.

15. (a.) The sign of Jonah was Jesus' last appeal to the Jews. Jesus compared Jonah's stay in the belly of the fish to the time he would be buried in the earth. Jesus knew the Jews had already rejected Him (Matthew 12:38–41).

16. (d.) It was after the Passover meal—not the traditional time for foot washing—that Jesus washed the disciples' feet. By performing this menial act, Jesus demonstrated the pattern for servanthood that was to distinguish the Christian life (John 13:2–20).

17. (a.) Paul was disturbed by the rampant idolatry in Athens. When he was invited to speak before an influential city council, Paul's opening remarks referred to the altar "To an Unknown God."

18. (d.) Jesus performed several miracles on the Sabbath (Mark 3:1–6; Luke 13:10–17; 14:1–24; John 5:1–17), an act offensive to the Pharisees. Jesus' explanation about His activities led to charges of blasphemy. No one incident triggered the Jews' hatred toward Jesus, but Sabbath-breaking, calling God

His Father, and equating Himself with God were among the most persistent charges (John 5:18–47; 10:30–31).

19. (c.) Changing water into wine at the wedding feast in Cana was the first of the thirty-five recorded miracles Jesus performed. The miracle at Cana was for a private audience and a specific purpose, namely to demonstrate Jesus' power to the men who had recently become His disciples (John 2:1–11).

20. (d.) Although there were large Jewish communities in Egypt and North Africa, Paul did not visit this region. Instead, his three missionary journeys took him to Galatia, Greece, and Asia Minor (Acts 13–14; 15:36–18:22; 18:23–21:14).

21. (c.) Matthew (21:9), Mark (11:9), and John (12:13) record parts of the simple "chorus" or praise hymn from Psalm 118:26 that was sung by the throngs as Jesus entered Jerusalem on Palm Sunday.

22. (a.) God chose a prophet, John the Baptist, to identify the prophetic roles of Jesus: first as the "lamb" of Leviticus 12 and Isaiah 53:7, and second, as the messianic Son of God (Psalm 2:7).

23. (d.) Matthew 16:17–19 tied Peter to a leadership role in the church. In Acts Peter led in the selection of Matthias (Acts 1:15–26), preached two powerful, post-Pentecost sermons (Acts 2:14–47; 3:11–26), was arrested for his theological assertions (Acts 4:1–4), amazed the religious hierarchy of the day (Acts 4:5–31), and dealt decisively with Ananias and Sapphira (Acts 5:1–11).

24. (d.) To all three temptations (Matthew 4:1–11), Jesus responded with statements from Deuteronomy (8:3; 6:13, 16; 10:20).

25. (b.) The disciples' questions prompted the "Olivet Discourse," which addressed the coming destruction of Jerusalem, the tribulation period, and Christ's second coming (Matthew 24–25; Mark 13; Luke 21:5–36).

26. (c.) Paul returned to Jerusalem in time for Pentecost (Acts 20:16), when the city teemed with international visitors. Asian Jews attacked Paul, nearly causing a riot (Acts 21:27–32). His resulting imprisonment fulfilled prophecy (Acts 21:8–14) and provided the opportunity for Paul to preach to several officials.

27. (b.) The verse, "Greater love has no one than this . . . " stemmed from the final instructions Jesus gave His disciples after the Last Supper (John 15:13).

28. (d.) Legally, the Jews were not permitted to execute anyone (although the Romans allowed them to kill any Gentile, including a Roman citizen, who entered the temple beyond the court of the Gentiles). Therefore, Caiaphas and the Sanhedrin were technically incapable of ordering the execution (John 18:31–32). Pilate, the procurator of Judea and Samaria, had sole responsibility for the courts in Jerusalem. When Pilate heard that Jesus was a Galilean and learned that Herod Antipas, the ruler of Galilee and Perea, was in Jerusalem, Pilate sent Jesus to Herod for sentencing. Herod mocked Jesus and returned Him to Pilate, who consented to the crucifixion (Luke 23:6–25).

29. (a.) Before Pentecost, nothing was noted about Joseph, the Levite from Cyprus. His nickname, "Barnabas," (son of encouragement), however, indicates that he was well known in the early church. Barnabas was generous with his possessions (Acts 4:36–37) and quick to affirm the ill-favored. He befriended the much-feared Saul (Acts 9:26–27) and later similarly supported his nephew, John Mark (Acts 15:36–39).

When persecution forced the early believers to scatter and the church at Antioch was formed, Barnabas was sent to investigate. At Antioch, Barnabas encouraged the believers and preached to the lost. Barnabas also maintained a heart for his homeland. On the first missionary journey, he and Paul "preached through" the island of Cyprus (Acts 13:4–6). When Barnabas and Paul later separated, Barnabas returned to Cyprus with John Mark (Acts 15:39).

30. (b.) Jesus' baptism was accompanied by a Triune validation that He was the Messiah. As an obedient Son, Jesus was baptized by John, the Holy Spirit filled Him for ministry, and the Father voiced His approval from heaven (Mark 1:9–11).

31. (a.) When Jesus taught on stewardship, He used the parable of the rich man and Lazarus. The story illustrated that righteousness stemmed from a belief in the words of Moses and the prophets (Luke 16:14, 19-31), not from wealth. The kingdom of heaven parables appear in Matthew 13.

32. (c.) After the Ascension, the disciples returned to Jerusalem and waited for what the Lord had promised. There, in the city poised for Pentecost, the Holy Spirit descended one morning (some time before 9:00 A.M.) and literally made the disciples witnesses to the people in Jerusalem, many of whom came from Judea and Samaria, and some from the remotest parts of the known world. Thus, the church was born (Acts 2:1–21).

33. (b.) Nicodemus—a Pharisee, a teacher, and a member of the elite Sanhedrin—probed Jesus about spiritual things one night. From that interview came the concise summary of the gospel, John 3:16, which is one of the most widely known New Testament verses. The Bible is silent about Nicodemus' own response to the meeting. Later, however, Nicodemus rebuked the Pharisees for judging Jesus without first hearing Him (John 7:50–51) and also supplied the spices for our Lord's burial (John 19:38–40).

34. (a.) Saul's conversion came as a result of a vision. On the road to Damascus Saul both heard and saw Jesus (Acts 9:3–6; 1 Corinthians 9:1). Years later Paul vividly recounted the event to the pagan King Agrippa (Acts 26:2–20).

35. (d.) Jesus challenged the people to repent and pursue righteousness (Matthew 4:17; Mark 1:15). Righteous living was the subject of His earliest major teaching, the Sermon on the Mount. Throughout His ministry Jesus spoke against a faith marked by hypocrisy.

36. (a.) Judas was in Gethsemane when Jesus was arrested. The subsequent trials that occurred during the night were illegal, yet by morning the Sanhedrin had essentially condemned Jesus. All that was needed for the execution was the Roman sanction. The turn of events surprised Judas, who probably killed himself while Jesus was being "examined" by Pilate and Herod (Matthew 27:1–5). Judas is not mentioned in the Gospels after the Crucifixion.

37. (c.) Paul loved the Ephesian elders. His poignant farewell (Acts 20:17–38) reveals the strong bond he felt for the men with whom he had shared the ministry of Jesus Christ.

38. (b.) The Scriptures bore witness to Jesus (John 5:39). Yet the New Testament repeatedly documents how those who "possessed" the law failed to believe it. At Jesus' birth, for in-

stance, the Magi stirred up the Jewish religious leaders, but they never investigated the wise men's claim. During Jesus' ministry, the religious Jews believed salvation came simply from a knowledge of Scripture rather than from an active belief. The Pharisees pitied the common man. They thought he was cursed because of his ignorance of the law (John 7:49).

39. (c.) According to Mark 11:1–17, Jesus cleansed the temple the day after His entry into Jerusalem. The act enraged the chief priests and scribes (Mark 11:18; Matthew 21:23–46) and stirred up their hatred for Him (Mark 14:1–2).

40. (a.) It was aboard ship on his way to Rome (approximately ten years after his second missionary journey) that Paul and his 276 companions were threatened by a raging, two-week long storm. Paul's calm manner was a testimony to his faith, and his wisdom preserved the lives of all on board (Acts 27).

41. (b.) After the Last Supper, Jesus crossed the Kidron and went to a garden called Gethsemane which He and His disciples had frequently visited (Luke 21:37; John 18:1). Gethsemane, which means "oil press," was a park-like, olive grove where visiting Jews to the city were accustomed to camping.

42. (c.) The Jews had tried to stone Jesus at the Feast of the Dedication, now known as Hanukkah. As a result, Jesus and the disciples went to Perea, the Roman province on the east side of the Jordan (John 10:22–40). When Jesus decided to return to Judea and possibly face the angry Jews, only Thomas was ready to "die with Him" (John 11:16).

43. (b.) Although Commander Lysias called Felix "the most excellent governor," Felix was known for his cruelty and spiritual indecision (Acts 24:24–27). Paul spent two years as a prisoner under his authority. Nero replaced Felix with Porcius Festus, who sought the help of King Agrippa in deciding Paul's case. Festus is most widely remembered as the man who called Paul "mad" (Acts 25:1–26:24).

44. (d.) Jesus warned the Pharisees and the scribes about their attitudes (Luke 11:37–54; John 8:12–59; Matthew 15:1–12). Even the disciples, who did not always track the significance of Jesus' teaching, were aware of the growing tension. As opposition increased, Jesus intensified the disciples' training

(Mark 6:30–32; 8:14–21; 9:9–13) and stressed the high cost of discipleship (Luke 9:57–62; Matthew 20:20–28).

45. (c.) The persecution of the church, which began in Acts 6:9 by the Synagogue of the Freedmen (which probably included Saul), exploded after Stephen's trial. The apostles were spared, but the Jerusalem church was scattered. Philip went to Samaria and other believers started the church at Antioch. Saul, a ringleader in the persecution, was on his way to imprison Christians when the Lord dramatically intervened (Acts 8:1–6; 9:1–8).

46. (c.) The synoptic Gospels reckoned time according to the Hebrews; sunrise (around 6:00 A.M.) was the first hour. Thus, the ninth hour corresponded to 3:00 P.M. Only the gospel of John (19:14) cited Roman time, which began at midnight.

47. (b.) After an orderly, spiritual assessment of the facts, the council at Jerusalem agreed that the Gentiles did not have to be circumcised in order to be saved. Instead, the council recommended that the Gentiles keep ceremonial food laws and refrain from fornication (Acts 15:19–29).

48. (c.) Matthew knew that tribal ancestry was important to the Jews. He carefully laid out Jesus' family tree, noting His tie to David, as evidence that Jesus was the Messiah (Matthew 1:3–16). In addition, Matthew quoted heavily from the Old Testament messianic prophecies to show their fulfillment in Jesus.

49. (b.) Although the term *deacon* is not mentioned in Acts 6, the precedent for the office of deacon was established when the apostles presented their division-of-labor solution to the Jerusalem church (Acts 6:1–6). The seven men chosen to assist the apostles have traditionally been called deacons. All seven had Greek names and were probably Hellenists (Greek-speaking Jews). Many Hellenists were converted on Pentecost and became part of the Jerusalem church, even though they could not speak Aramaic. Since the conflict in the church arose over the issue of food for the Hellenist widows, it was prudent that the deacons chosen should identify with the needs of the slighted minority.

The qualifications for the first deacons were simple: "men of good reputation, full of the Spirit and of wisdom" (Acts 6:3).

They seemed to encapsulate the more specific requirements later called out in 1 Timothy 3:8–13.

50. (d.) John and Jesus met infrequently in Scripture, but their lives were bound together before their births. John's mother, Elizabeth, and Jesus' mother, Mary, were related (Luke 1:36). Both men were prophets. John the Baptist was the forerunner of Jesus (Malachi 3:1; Mark 1:2–3). This is in keeping with John's name, since the term *Baptist*, means "identifier." John baptized Jesus and developed his image as the "friend of the bridegroom" (John 3:27–36).

SEVEN

THE EPISTLES

IT WAS A MORNING WHEN NOTHING WENT RIGHT. The commuter crowds spilled out of Union Station and oozed toward Lake MIchigan. At the outer edges of the moving mass, a lone figure stopped, checked a map, and searched for landmarks. A droop in the shoulders was the only indication that she had miscalculated the human traffic flow and ended up on the wrong street. The mistake would make her late.

Clutching a packet marked "WRITER'S CONFERENCE— Moody Bible Institute, Chicago, Illinois," she maneuvered toward Wacker Drive and queued up at the light.

Through the waiting legs shifting nervously on the curb, she spied a single phrase, spray-painted on the concrete in black scribble: *Trust Jesus.* It seemed out of place, a desecration to walk on. She cringed for the indignity it imparted.

Falling in with the cadence of the workaday gladiators, she crossed the street and marched through the towering corridors of office glass and steel. She rounded the curve by the Apparel Mart, and, for the first time, noticed the crowds had thinned.

She could slow down. She wanted to slow down. No, what she really wanted was to go home.

This was Tuesday, and today she was going to have to admit she was a "beginner."

Monday, the opening day of the writer's conference, was filled with special events, but Tuesday through Friday the morning agenda included graded, continuing classes. It was the graded part that made her cringe. If you had never published, you were a beginner.

It was tough to be a beginner. Life was a parade of anxiety, mistakes, and awkwardness. Children-beginners were compensated; they were encouraged. But adult beginners only evoked questions: "You want to do what!" "How can you compete?" "Aren't you happy?"

Tuesday promised even more discomfort. The conference had invited attendees to submit manuscripts for professional review. She had submitted two, a book proposal and a magazine article. It was her first proposal. For that matter, it was her first article. She had even included its cover letter for evaluation.

She smiled weakly. Nobody "professional" would ask for help with a letter.

She marched beside the Chicago River, Fear before her, Desire-to-Write behind. Fear punched and counter-punched; "Go home. Go home." Yet, Desire-to-Write propelled her ahead.

She didn't feel well. Her breakfast lumped. Her lungs constricted. Her armpits stuck together.

She breathed a "deep, cleansing breath," a relaxation technique gleaned from bygone childbirth classes, but hot street fumes triggered nausea. The breakfast lump rose like an express elevator and lodged at the tonsils.

"You are on the verge of a public nervous breakdown," her inner voice croaked. With breakfast bulging in her throat, she dismissed the breakdown.

Somewhere, a distant clock gonged eight.

Decidedly late, she rounded the corner onto LaSalle Street.

There, on a post in the same offensive spray-paint scrawl, was "*Trust Jesus.*"

The reminder wasn't even punctuated!

She didn't care.

She drank in the message.

It anointed her head and trickled over her body; she was glazed, immersed in truth like a chocolate-covered strawberry. For brief seconds, time held no sway.

She was safe.

The lump dissolved. The lungs relaxed. Fear vanished. Desire stopped pushing. A new motivator spurred her on: Jesus.

Jesus was more than capable of guiding her through the intricacies of publishing hoops. Her ministry was in His hands; obedience to the opportunities was in hers.

The heavens declare the glory of God. Periodically, people do, too. She thanked God for the writer He commissioned to "graffiti His glory" on public places. His two-word theology restored her soul.

The writer in this story didn't have time for "deep theology." Fear, uncertainty, and pride were strangling her spiritual equilibrium. Yet, two words shifted the balance. All she knew, all she believed, was reduced to a reminder: Trust Jesus.

The New Testament epistles were written to people exactly like this writer: Christians under fire.

Epistles are often thought of as weighty doctrine, but they really are reminders, personal messages to ordinary people facing issues as practical as the writer's crippling fear. The epistles do teach doctrine and emphasize theology. But doctrine and theology serve to nudge believers about their behavior.

When it comes to behavior, the epistles don't mince words: "be imitators of God"; "Have this attitude in yourselves which was also in Christ Jesus"; "walk by the Spirit." In short, the writers of the epistles ask one thing: curb behavior. Their commands are simple and childlike: "Bless those who persecute you," "Love one another," and "do not grow weary of doing good."

Each major division of the Bible equips the reader in a unique way. The historical books inform us about God. The poetical books show us how to respond to Him. The prophetical books permit us to glimpse His power. In this last major division of the New Testament, the epistles remind us to act like Christ.

Questions

1. An epistle is
   a. a letter.
   b. a short, pithy saying.
   c. a figure of speech.

d. a journal.

2. The epistle that exhorts its readers to think about "whatever is true," "honorable," "right," "lovely," "worthy of praise" is

    a. Ephesians.
    b. Philippians.
    c. Colossians.
    d. Romans.

3. The purpose of the New Testament epistle was to

    a. instruct and encourage believers in the Christian faith.
    b. explain the miracles to the churches.
    c. expose human folly.
    d. record history.

4. The church which was geographically closest to the Colossian church was at

    a. Thessalonica.
    b. Corinth.
    c. Ephesus.
    d. Philippi.

5. Titus and Timothy were both

    a. tentmakers.
    b. Roman officers.
    c. elders at the Antioch church.
    d. pastors.

6. The statement that best summarizes the epistle of James is:

    a. genuine faith produces visible works.
    b. the Crucifixion is central to Christianity.
    c. false teachers exist in the church body.
    d. the Holy Spirit gives spiritual gifts to the church.

7. The shortest of the following Epistles is

    a. 1 John.

b. 1 Corinthians.

c. 3 John.

d. James.

8. The requirements for elders (bishops) and deacons are most clearly set forth in

a. Hebrews.

b. 1 Timothy and Titus.

c. James.

d. Ephesians and Colossians.

9. The writer who did not write a "general" epistle was

a. John.

b. Jude.

c. Paul.

d. Peter.

10. According to Paul, what is patient, kind, not jealous, does not brag, . . . bears all things, believes all things, endures all things, and never fails?

a. Love

b. Faith

c. Hope

d. All of the above

11. The epistle that appears first in the New Testament canon is

a. Galatians.

b. Romans.

c. 1 Corinthians.

d. 1 Timothy.

12. In the New Testament _____ books are epistles.

a. nine

b. thirteen

c. five

d. twenty-two

13. Literary techniques found in the Epistles include
    a. figurative language.
    b. repetition.
    c. parallelism.
    d. all of the above.

14. The epistle which places Scripture—inspired by God and profitable for teaching—at the center of the Christian's ministry is
    a. James.
    b. Romans.
    c. 2 Timothy.
    d. Philemon.

15. The "Heroes Hall of Fame," a list of Old Testament saints who demonstrated faith, is found in
    a. Hebrews.
    b. Romans.
    c. Philemon.
    d. none of the above.

16. The *body* of an epistle contains doctrine (teaching) and
    a. the writer's name.
    b. application or exhortation.
    c. final greetings.
    d. travel instructions.

17. Tychicus, Aristarchus, and Epaphroditus were
    a. believers who ministered to Paul in prison.
    b. the elders of the Corinthian church.
    c. false prophets.
    d. government officials.

18. The redemptive story line begun in Genesis is finished by John in his epistle,
    a. 1 John.
    b. 2 John.

    c. 3 John.

    d. Revelation.

19. The epistle that follows Romans is

    a. 1 Corinthians.

    b. Colossians.

    c. Philippians.

    d. none of the above.

20. The two epistles that focus on end time events and urge Christlike behavior while waiting are

    a. 1, 2 Timothy.

    b. 1, 2 Thessalonians.

    c. 1, 2 Corinthians.

    d. Colossians and Philippians.

21. "For by grace you have been saved through faith; and that not of yourselves, it is the gift of God; not as a result of works, that no one should boast. For we are His workmanship, created in Christ Jesus for good works, which God prepared beforehand, that we should walk in them."

    The preceding passage is from

    a. 1 Peter.

    b. Hebrews.

    c. Ephesians.

    d. 1 John.

22. The epistle known for its proverbs, such as "prove yourselves doers of the word, and not merely hearers" and "Draw near to God and He will draw near to you," is

    a. Hebrews.

    b. James.

    c. 2 Corinthians.

    d. Jude.

23. The longest Pauline epistle is

    a. Romans.

   b. Galatians.

   c. 2 Timothy.

   d. Philemon.

24. The superiority of Christ over the prophets, the angels, and Moses is emphasized in

   a. Romans.

   b. 1 Corinthians.

   c. 2 Corinthians.

   d. Hebrews.

25. The "general" Epistles were written by _____ different writers.

   a. nine

   b. seven

   c. five

   d. three

26. Practical church problems, such as divisions in the body, incest, lawsuits, marriage versus singleness, and the abuse of the Lord's Supper, are examined in

   a. Romans.

   b. Revelation.

   c. Philemon.

   d. 1 Corinthians.

27. Symbols such as the Lamb, four horsemen, a book with seven seals, lampstands, and a great red dragon are widely used in

   a. Romans.

   b. Revelation.

   c. 1 Thessalonians.

   d. Jude.

28. The epistle that follows Hebrews is

   a. 1 Peter.

   b. 1 John.

   c. James.

d. Jude.

29. Nine of Paul's epistles are written to

    a. local churches.
    b. the Christian public at large.
    c. fellow missionaries/evangelists.
    d. individual believers.

30. "And I saw heaven opened; and behold, a white horse, and He who sat upon it is called Faithful and True; and in righteousness He judges and wages war. . . . And He is clothed with a robe dipped in blood; and His name is called The Word of God."

    The author of the above passage is

    a. Peter.
    b. the writer of Hebrews.
    c. Paul.
    d. John.

31. The New Testament Epistles were written between

    a. 20 B.C.–30 A.D.
    b. 1–30 A.D.
    c. 45–95 A.D.
    d. 100–200 A.D.

32. The pre-eminence of Christ in all things and the behavior of those who have set their "mind on the things above, not on the things that are on earth" is discussed in

    a. Romans.
    b. Galatians.
    c. 1 Corinthians.
    d. Colossians.

33. "Therefore, since we have so great a cloud of witnesses surrounding us, let us also lay aside every encumbrance, and the sin which so easily entangles us, and let us run with

endurance the race that is set before us, fixing our eyes on Jesus."

The author of the above verse was

a. Peter.
b. the writer of Hebrews.
c. Paul.
d. John.

34. The last epistle written was

a. Ephesians.
b. Revelation.
c. Romans.
d. James.

35. "Have this attitude in yourselves which was also in Christ Jesus, who, although He existed in the form of God, did not regard equality with God a thing to be grasped, but emptied Himself, taking the form of a bond-servant, and being made in the likeness of men."

Paul makes this exhortation to a church in the epistle to

a. Titus.
b. 2 Timothy.
c. Philippians.
d. Philemon.

36. 1 Peter was written to believers who were

a. suffering persecution for their faith.
b. leaders of large churches.
c. fearful they had missed the Second Coming of Jesus.
d. untaught about spiritual gifts.

37. Paul speaks of the mystery of the gospel, the mystery of Christ and the Gentiles, the mystery of the resurrection of the saints, and the mystery of Christ and the church. Paul's definition of a New Testament "mystery" is

a. an unsolvable riddle.

b. a truth known only to the Apostles.

c. a truth hidden in the past but revealed in the New Testament times.

d. a contradiction.

38. Paul defended his character, his conduct, and his calling as an apostle before the church at

    a. Thessalonica.

    b. Corinth.

    c. Philippi.

    d. Colossae.

39. *Abba* was

    a. a term of endearment meaning "Daddy."

    b. a first century philosophy.

    c. a once-trusted disciple who abandoned his faith.

    d. a first century deaconess.

40. Paul begins each of his epistles with the word or phrase

    a. "Grace to you."

    b. "Paul."

    c. "To the saints."

    d. "I thank my God."

41. The phrase, "It is a trustworthy statement" (NAS), or "This is a faithful saying" (KJV), is used repeatedly in

    a. Romans.

    b. Ephesians.

    c. 1 Timothy.

    d. James.

42. In Paul's shortest epistle, he attempts to restore harmony between a master and his slave. The epistle is

    a. Titus.

    b. 1 Timothy.

    c. 2 Timothy.

    d. Philemon.

43. The Pauline epistles are generally arranged according to

    a. the order in which they were first written.
    b. decreasing length.
    c. increasing length.
    d. alphabetical order.

44. "I felt the necessity to write to you appealing that you contend earnestly for the faith which was once for all delivered to the saints. For certain persons have crept in unnoticed, those who were long beforehand marked out for this condemnation, ungodly persons who turn the grace of our God into licentiousness and deny our only Master and Lord, Jesus Christ."

    The above passage was written by

    a. Jude.
    b. James.
    c. the writer of Hebrews.
    d. Paul.

45. The epistle that *precedes* 1 Thessalonians is

    a. 2 Corinthians.
    b. Philippians.
    c. Colossians.
    d. Ephesians.

46. Sometimes called the "little Romans," the epistle which denounces legalism and teaches justification by faith alone is

    a. Ephesians.
    b. 1 Thessalonians.
    c. Galatians.
    d. 1 Timothy.

47. Which of the following verses is found in 2 Peter?

    a. "No one can tame the tongue; it is a restless evil and full of deadly poison."

b. "The Lord is not slow about His promise, as some count slowness, but is patient toward you, not wishing for any to perish but for all to come to repentance. But the day of the Lord will come."

c. "To live is Christ, and to die is gain."

d. "I have no greater joy than this, to hear of my children walking in the truth."

48. The first epistle Paul wrote was

a. Galatians.
b. 1 Timothy.
c. Titus.
d. Philemon.

49. Which of the following verses does *not* appear in 1 John?

a. "Little children, let us not love with word or with tongue, but in deed and truth."

b. "See how great a love the Father has bestowed upon us, that we should be called children of God."

c. "[B]ut if we walk in the light as He Himself is in the light, we have fellowship with one another, and the blood of Jesus His Son cleanses us from all sin."

d. "Jesus Christ is the same yesterday and today, yes and forever."

50. In the epistles, the "benediction" is usually found

a. in the opening greeting.
b. in the doctrinal section.
c. in the closing.
d. never in the epistles.

Answers

1. (a.) The terms *epistle* and *letter* are often used interchangeably, but, strictly speaking, a first century epistle was a

formal letter written to be read aloud or publicly posted. Classic examples are 1 John and 2 Peter. A letter, on the other hand, was personal communication which privately addressed issues. Thus 1 Corinthians and Philemon are true letters. In spite of some differences, the epistle and the letter share a common form. Both have an opening, a section of thanksgiving, a well-defined body, and a final greeting with a farewell.

2. (b.) Philippians 4:8 provided thoughtful suggestions to counter discord in the church and to nurture Christ-like behavior.

3. (a.) The format of an epistle lends itself to both instruction and encouragement.

4. (c.) Colossae was about 100 miles east of Ephesus. Paul wrote Colossians and Ephesians at the same time, and Tychicus delivered them to the churches (Colossians 4:7; Ephesians 6:21).

5. (d.) Timothy pastored a church in Ephesus; Titus, a Gentile convert, ministered on the island of Crete.

6. (a.) Whether facing trials or taming the tongue, James teaches that genuine faith produces visible changes in attitude and action. James makes no mention of the church, spiritual gifts, or the Crucifixion.

7. (c.) John's short "note" to the "beloved Gaius" would have fit nicely on the traditional stationery of the day, a sheet of ancient papyrus measuring ten by eight inches.

8. (b.) Who needed insight on selecting leadership? Pastors. So it was to Pastor Timothy and Pastor Titus that Paul supplied the written guidelines for elders and deacons.

9. (c.) Paul wrote nine letters to churches and four to individuals. He wrote none of the general epistles.

10. (a.) According to 1 Corinthians 13:4–8, love is patient, kind, etc. 1 Corinthians 13 is known as the "love" chapter.

11. (b.) Romans is the first epistle in the New Testament canon.

12. (d.) The New Testament contains twenty-two epistles; thirteen are Pauline and nine are general.

13. (d.) The epistles belong to "occasional" literature, writing prompted by an event or circumstance. Epistles are prose, but letter writers communicated abstract ideas by using the

poet's tools. Figurative language led Peter to describe the spiritual condition of false teachers: "They are springs without water" (2 Peter 2:17). Repetition emphasized ideas: "There is one body and one Spirit, just as also you were called in one hope of your calling; one Lord, one faith, one baptism, one God and Father of all who is over all and through all and in all" (Ephesians 4:4–6). Parallelism helped describe the bond between Christ and the believer: "For I am convinced that neither death, nor life, nor angels, nor principalities, nor things present, nor things to come, nor powers, nor height, nor depth, nor any other created thing, shall be able to separate us from the love of God, which is in Christ Jesus our Lord" (Romans 8:38–39).

14. (c.) 2 Timothy proclaims the importance of Scripture. In fact, the book is filled with synonyms for Scripture: "the testimony of our Lord" (1:8), "the gospel" (1:10), "the standard of sound words" (1:13), "the word of God" (2:9), "the word of truth" (2:15), "the firm foundation of God" (2:19), and "the sacred writings" (3:15).

15. (a.) Heroes of the faith are listed in Hebrews 11.

16. (b.) The body of an epistle weds doctrine to exhortation or application. Epistle writers taught first and then exhorted. Alert readers will notice that the word *therefore* often separates the doctrinal and the exhortative sections. (For examples, see Romans 12:1; Ephesians 4:1; Philippians 2:1, and Hebrews 12:1.)

17. (a.) These three men ministered to Paul in Rome during his imprisonment. Tychicus and Aristarchus were mentioned in Colossians 4; Epaphroditus was commended in Philippians 2.

18. (d.) The redemption promised in Genesis reaches its culmination in Revelation. Revelation brims with details about the final judgment, Satan's defeat, and the rule and the reign of believers with Jesus Christ. Chapter 19 is particularly glorious. It describes the marriage supper of the Lamb, truly an event of inexpressible joy for believers.

19. (a.) 1 Corinthians follows Romans.

20. (b.) Even though the letters to the Thessalonians mention nearly every doctrine, the thrust of the messages was instruction and comfort about Jesus' return. These epistles, along

with the Olivet Discourse and portions of 2 Peter and Revelation, constitute the major prophetic texts of the New Testament.

21. (c.) The lyric assurance found in the epistle to the Ephesians (2:8–10) stands in sharp contrast to Revelation 2:4 where this same Ephesian church is "charged" with leaving its first love.

22. (b.) James is known as the "proverbs" of the New Testament. James' proverbs intrude on our thoughts long after they have been read. Jesus, too, used these pithy sayings to trigger the imagination: "You are the salt of the earth" (Matthew 5:13).

23. (a.) Romans is not only the longest of Paul's epistles, it is by far the most formal. Since Paul did not know the church body at Rome, the letter does not correct or reprove the congregation. Instead, Romans offers sound, systematic teaching on the basics of the faith, particularly the doctrines of sin and salvation.

24. (d.) Christ's superiority is heralded in Hebrews.

25. (c.) Five writers wrote the nine general Epistles. The apostle John wrote four books; Peter wrote two. James, Jude, and the writer of Hebrews each wrote one.

26. (d.) Both letters to the Corinthians addressed a wide range of practical issues affecting church relationships and Christian lifestyles.

27. (b.) Revelation bulges with symbols, images which represent characters and events in the closing chapters of world history.

28. (c.) James follows Hebrews.

29. (a.) Paul wrote nine epistles to local churches. Part teacher, part exhorter, part encourager, part visionary, Paul fervently promoted churches. While writing to the Corinthians, he admitted: "I am jealous for you with a godly jealousy; for I betrothed you to one husband, that to Christ I might present you as a pure virgin" (2 Corinthians 11:2).

30. (d.) John had been instructed in Revelation 1:19 to "Write . . . the things which shall take place." Amid the calamities, he recorded the passage about the second coming of Christ (19:11–21).

31. (c.) The Epistles were written after Pentecost. Most scholars place Galatians and James, the earliest letters, around 45 A.D., and Revelation, the last letter, about 95 A.D.

32. (d.) Christ's pre-eminence is proclaimed in Colossians, a letter written to a "small town" church that Paul never saw!

33. (b.) After eleven chapters of heavy theology, historical references, and Old Testament symbols, the writer of Hebrews sets the changeless Christ before his readers as the focus of their entire life's "race" (12:1–2).

34. (b.) Revelation, the last book of the Bible, was also the last epistle written.

35. (c.) To the Philippian church, ailing from chronic grumbling, Paul held high Jesus' example of servanthood as the banner for church unity (2:5–7).

36. (a.) 1 Peter focused on external forces affecting the church. The apostle urged those suffering persecution for their faith to lead godly lives.

37. (c.) In the Epistles, Paul comments on a number of spiritual truths which were once concealed from men but are now made known because of Christ. Here are a few of Paul's mysteries: the mystery of the gospel (Romans 16:25), the mystery of Christ and the Gentiles (Ephesians 3:3–7), the mystery of Christ and the church (Ephesians 5:32).

38. (b.) After false teachers used 1 Corinthians to challenge Paul's authority, Titus was dispatched to quell the furor. While most of the people responded favorably to Titus, a small number in the church still opposed Paul. In 2 Corinthians Paul defends himself, and we glimpse the human side of Paul: his trials, his personality, and his frustrations.

39. (a.) *Abba* was the Aramaic word for "Daddy." Jesus used the word as He prayed to His Father in Gethsemane (Mark 14:36). Because of the intimate overtones, the Jews never addressed God as Abba. It is significant that Paul links the word with salvation and encourages Christians to use the term to reinforce their spiritual relationship with God the Father (Romans 8:15; Galatians 4:6).

40. (b.) Each of Paul's epistles begins with the word *Paul.*

41. (c.) The phrase "It is a trustworthy statement" is characteristic of 1 Timothy, although it is used once in each of the other pastoral epistles.

42. (d.) In Philemon, more of a personal memo than a full-fledged letter, Paul demonstrates how the love of Christ can erase social distinctions and soothe rebellious attitudes.

43. (b.) The Pauline epistles are generally ordered according to decreasing length, beginning with Romans, the longest letter, and ending with Philemon, the shortest.

44. (a.) In plain language Jude sounds the alarm about false teachers who distort the gospel. Jude is not entirely glum, however. His benediction (24–25) offers encouragement and reassurance.

45. (c.) Colossians precedes 1 Thesslaonians and joins with Ephesians, Philippians, and Philemon to form what is commonly called the "prison" epistles.

46. (c.) Galatians, which has impacted Christianity throughout the ages, denounces legalism and teaches justification by faith, not by works. This epistle was so dear to Martin Luther that he referred to it as his "wife."

47. (b.) 2 Peter focused on internal forces affecting the church. The aging apostle sought to warn and allay the believers' fears about the increasing heresies in the church. Peter was confident that, in spite of "public opinion," God would intervene in human affairs just as He had in the days of Noah.

48. (a.) Paul wrote his first letters to churches, not to individuals. Galatians was probably written between the end of Paul's first missionary journey and the Jerusalem council on Gentile circumcision.

49. (d.) "Jesus Christ is the same yesterday and today, yes and forever" is taken from Hebrews 13:8.

50. (c.) Like this question, the benediction closes the epistle.

EIGHT

BIBLE PERSONALITIES

WHO IS CHRISTOPHER BRASHER?

On May 6, 1954, three runners from Oxford University set out to break a world record. Only one succeeded, but, as a team, the men swept race honors, finishing first, second, and third. Sports fans still thrill to the grainy black-and-white footage of the final meters of the competition. Yet only the winner is remembered.

With his official time of 3:59.4, Roger Bannister was the first human to run a sub-four-minute mile. Teammate Christopher Chataway missed immortality by seven seconds. Their cohort, Christopher Brasher, was officially declared third. However, scorers and officials were so distracted by Bannister's performance that no one even recorded Brasher's time!

Life seems to offer "starring" roles and "supporting" roles for people to play.

Who dropped the bomb on Nagasaki?

Historians answer: the United States. Politicians quip: Harry Truman.

The man who actually dropped the atomic bomb on Nagasaki was Army Air Corps bombardier Kermit Beahan, a man who played a deciding part in world history and then quietly moved on.

In Scripture there is only one starring role; it belongs to Jesus. Whether He is the Promise set before Adam or the Lamb set before the elders of Revelation, the Bible magnifies Jesus Christ.

Jesus is revealed against a backdrop of biblical history, which showcases nearly three thousand human "supporting" roles. There is the choleric David, the comely Esther, mighty Samson, old Methuselah, fat Eglon, love-struck Jacob, wicked kings, arrogant conquerors, sorrowful prophets, the barren, the mourners, and the obedient.

"Bible Personalities" looks at some of the people who played supporting roles in Scripture. The focus of the chapter is not on the famous but on the fleeting: those wives or children, prophets or priests, friends or enemies who dart through the pages of the Bible and move history forward. The lives of the characters selected illustrate spiritual principles: faith, loyalty, obedience, or duty. Step now through the expanse of Scripture, looking at the Bible personalities whose supporting roles helped to shape God's revelation and our faith.

Questions

1. The "king of Salem" was

    a. Melchizedek.
    b. Abimelech.
    c. Chedorlaomer.
    d. Lot.

2. The only disciple whom Jesus directly asked, "Do you love me?" was

    a. John.
    b. Peter.
    c. James.
    d. Thomas.

3. Solomon's mother's name was

    a. Ahinoam the Jezreelitess.
    b. Michal.
    c. Bathsheba.
    d. Abigail.

4. The aging but vigorous soldier who inherited Hebron was

   a. Joshua.
   b. Caleb.
   c. Ehud.
   d. Othniel.

5. Abigail's first husband was

   a. Nabal.
   b. Jonathan.
   c. Joab.
   d. Abner.

6. Paul's first European convert was

   a. Dorcas.
   b. Lydia.
   c. Priscilla.
   d. Eunice.

7. Philip, Bartholomew, Thomas, James the son of Alphaeus, Thaddeus, and Simon the Zealot were all

   a. elders of the churches in Asia.
   b. people healed by Jesus.
   c. deacons.
   d. apostles.

8. "You shall separate everyone who laps the water with his tongue, as a dog laps, as well as everyone who kneels to drink." The judge who was told this was

   a. Othniel.
   b. Samson.
   c. Gideon.
   d. Jephthah.

9. The standard for judging the subsequent kings of Judah was measured by the conduct of

   a. Saul.
   b. David.

c. Solomon.

d. Josiah.

10. The man mentioned by name the most times in the New Testament is

   a. Pontius Pilate.

   b. Luke.

   c. Matthew.

   d. Timothy.

11. The first and second kings of Israel were anointed by

   a. Zadok.

   b. Abiathar.

   c. Samuel.

   d. Eli.

12. David's best friend as a young man was

   a. Barzillai.

   b. Mephibosheth.

   c. Abner.

   d. Jonathan.

13. When Jesus said, "I am the resurrection and the life; he who believes in Me shall live even if he dies, and everyone who lives and believes in Me shall never die," He was speaking to

   a. Martha.

   b. His mother, Mary.

   c. the Samaritan woman at the well.

   d. Elizabeth.

14. The prophet who ate a book was

   a. Isaiah.

   b. Ezekiel.

   c. Elijah.

   d. Daniel.

15. "How long will you hesitate between two opinions? If the Lord is God follow Him; but if Baal, follow him." This was said on Mount Carmel by

    a. Elijah.
    b. Hezekiah.
    c. Elisha.
    d. Balak.

16. The first century Christians known for their serious study of the Scriptures were the

    a. Thessalonians.
    b. Cretans.
    c. Galatians.
    d. Bereans.

17. The Moabites and the Ammonites were descended from

    a. Laban.
    b. Lot.
    c. Esau.
    d. Ishmael.

18. Queen of the Southern Kingdom of Judah was

    a. Athaliah.
    b. Sheba.
    c. Esther.
    d. Jezebel.

19. The king of Palestine when Jesus was born was

    a. Herod the Great.
    b. Herod Antipas.
    c. Herod Agrippa I.
    d. Herod Agrippa II.

20. Given an inheritance in the Promised Land along with Jacob's sons were the sons of

    a. Esau.
    b. Levi.

c. Joseph.

d. Ishmael.

21. The general of Israel's army was David's nephew,

    a. Asahel.

    b. Joab.

    c. Ish-bosheth.

    d. Abishai.

22. According to Matthew 1, the king *not* in the lineage of Jesus was

    a. Uzziah.

    b. Asa.

    c. Saul.

    d. Hezekiah.

23. The woman who prayed so fervently that Eli thought she was drunk was

    a. Hannah.

    b. Peninnah.

    c. Ruth.

    d. Manoah's wife.

24. "If they do not listen to Moses and the Prophets, neither will they be persuaded if someone rises from the dead." In the parable of Lazarus and the rich man, this is a quote from

    a. the rich man.

    b. Lazarus.

    c. Abraham.

    d. Moses.

25. The husband of Jezebel was

    a. Ahab.

    b. Omri.

    c. Jeroboam.

    d. Zimri.

26. The affliction of Bartimaeus that Jesus healed was

    a. demons.
    b. leprosy.
    c. a severed ear.
    d. blindness.

27. After the Exile, when the temple was rebuilt, the high priest was

    a. Jeshua or Joshua.
    b. Nehemiah.
    c. Zerubbabel.
    d. Sanballat.

28. Laban's eldest daughter was

    a. Bilhah.
    b. Rachel.
    c. Zilpah.
    d. Leah.

29. The Gospel of Luke and the Acts of the Apostles were specifically addressed to

    a. Rufus.
    b. the dearly beloved in Christ.
    c. Theophilus.
    d. the saints at Rome.

30. The person stricken with leprosy for complaining and murmuring was

    a. Miriam.
    b. Naaman.
    c. Gehazi.
    d. Uzziah.

31. The son of David who attempted to take over his kingdom was

    a. Amnon.
    b. Absalom.

c. Adonijah.
d. Chileab.

32. In the Gospels, Joseph of Arimathea's role was that he

a. brought spices to Jesus' burial.
b. helped Jesus carry the cross.
c. removed Jesus' body from the Cross and placed it in his own tomb.
d. was the Roman centurion whose faith amazed Jesus.

33. The request, "Please, let a double portion of your spirit be upon me," was made by

a. Joshua.
b. Gehazi.
c. Elisha.
d. Elijah.

34. After making a rash vow, _____ defeated the Ammonites?

a. Ehud.
b. Jephthah.
c. Othniel.
d. Gideon.

35. "Why has Satan filled your heart to lie to the Holy Spirit, and to keep back some of the price of the land?" In this quotation Peter was speaking to

a. Ananias.
b. Joseph Justus.
c. Elymas.
d. Eutychus.

36. Methuselah's famous grandson was

a. Melchizedek.
b. Noah.
c. Enoch.
d. Abraham.

37. The gifted preacher instructed by Priscilla and Aquila was

    a. Apollos.
    b. Timothy.
    c. Peter.
    d. Philip.

38. Rabshakeh was

    a. the king spared by Saul but executed by Samuel.
    b. the king who sent cedars from Lebanon.
    c. an Assyrian military officer under Sennacherib.
    d. a Syrian army captain healed of leprosy.

39. The queen who instituted Purim was

    a. Candace.
    b. Michal.
    c. Vashti.
    d. Esther.

40. Abner was

    a. David's high priest.
    b. Saul's chief general.
    c. Michal's second husband.
    d. Saul's youngest son.

41. Jesus was anointed with expensive perfume a week before His death by

    a. Mary of Bethany.
    b. Mary, the mother of John Mark.
    c. Mary Magdalene.
    d. Mary, the mother of James.

42. The craftsman in charge of building the tabernacle was

    a. Korah.
    b. Joshua.
    c. Jethro.
    d. Bezalel.

43. The high priest who took part in the trials of Jesus, Peter, and John was

    a. Zacharias.
    b. Gamaliel.
    c. Annas.
    d. Nicodemus.

44. *Not* among David's mighty men of valor was

    a. Abishai.
    b. Asahel.
    c. Uriah the Hittite.
    d. Ahithophel.

45. The woman Peter raised from the dead in Joppa was

    a. Dorcas.
    b. Euodia.
    c. Phoebe.
    d. Syntyche.

46. Jacob's youngest son was

    a. Joseph.
    b. Judah.
    c. Levi.
    d. Benjamin.

47. The first woman to be called a "wife" was

    a. Sarah.
    b. Noah's wife.
    c. Eve.
    d. Lot's wife.

48. "He received a rebuke for his own transgression; for a dumb donkey, speaking with a voice of a man, restrained the madness of the prophet." In this passage Peter was referring to

    a. the false prophet of the Tribulation.
    b. Balaam.

    c. Hananiah.

    d. Elymas.

49. The man who died as he attempted to steady the ark of God was

    a. Eli.

    b. Obed-edom.

    c. Uzzah.

    d. Phinehas.

50. "If anyone takes away from the words of the book of this prophecy, God shall take away his part from the tree of life and from the holy city, which are written in this book." This warning was written by

    a. Jude.

    b. Peter.

    c. Paul.

    d. John.

Answers

1. (a.) Little is known about Melchizedek, the king of Salem. Genesis 14:18–20 identifies him historically. Psalm 110:4 views him prophetically. Hebrews 5–7 compares his priesthood to Christ's. Scripture portrays Melchizedek as a type of Christ.

2. (b.) Three times Jesus questioned Peter's love. The encounter followed a postresurrection breakfast on the shores of the Sea of Galilee, where Jesus talked about Peter's responsibility and personal destiny and requested Peter's obedience (John 21:15–22). Jesus' three questions offered Peter the opportunity to offset his three earlier denials of Christ and to reaffirm his faith.

3. (c.) Bathsheba was the mother of Solomon, who was the second child produced by the union of King David and the beautiful queen (2 Samuel 12:15–19; 24–25). Before David's death, Bathsheba joined with Nathan the prophet to bring about Solomon's coronation (1 Kings 1:11–31). Bathsheba is identified indirectly in the genealogy of Christ (Matthew 1:6).

4. (b.) Hebron belonged to Caleb, who at age eighty-five vowed to rid the land of the giants he had seen forty-five years earlier as a spy (Joshua 14:6–14). Caleb is one of the rare Biblical examples of active, steadfast godliness in old age.

5. (a.) Nabal, whose name means "fool," was Abigail's first husband. His surly disposition and inhospitable acts stand in contrast to Abigail's gracious quick-wittedness and godly goodwill (1 Samuel 25:2–38).

6. (b.) Lydia was the first convert Paul made after his arrival in Greece (Acts 16:14). Lydia was a successful Gentile merchant who opened her home to Paul, Silas, Timothy, and Luke, as well as local believers (Acts 16:15, 40). Paul's first convert in Asia was Epaenetus (Romans 16:5).

7. (d.) The men were six of the twelve apostles (Mark 3:14–19; Luke 6:12–16). Although Scripture paints detailed portraits of a few apostles, the personalities of most of the Twelve remain a mystery. Unfortunately, tradition, Medieval mysticism, and spiritual serendipity have assigned traits and miracles to many of the lesser known apostles that Scripture does not corroborate.

8. (c.) Exactly why Gideon's men were selected by this peculiar, time-consuming test is not known (Judges 7:1–6). One of the scripturally consistent explanations is that Baal worshipers customarily bowed their knees in worship (1 Kings 19:18), while the Jews prostrated themselves before Jehovah. Thus the men would have revealed whom they customarily worshiped by how they drank the water. Gideon and the three hundred men routed a much larger Midianite army.

9. (b.) David became the standard against which the kingships of Judah were judged. Solomon's failure to be "wholly devoted to the Lord his God, as the heart of David his father had been" resulted in the division of the kingdom (1 Kings 11:4, 11–13). From that point forward, many of Judah's kings, including Rehoboam (2 Chronicles 11:17), Abijam (1 Kings 15:3), Jehoshaphat (2 Chronicles 17:3), Hezekiah (2 Kings 18:3), and Josiah (2 Kings 22:2), were compared to David.

10. (a.) The bad as well as the good are featured in Scripture. Pilate's name appears fifty-six times in the New Testament. He is mentioned in all four Gospels, the book of Acts,

and in one epistle. Pilate is mentioned twice as often as Timothy, eleven times as often as Matthew or Mark, and twenty-eight times as often as Luke. Even John, the most mentioned gospel writer, is not cited as often as Pilate.

11. (c.) Samuel anointed both Saul and David, although he did not live to see David crowned (1 Samuel 9:15–10:1; 16:12–13). In addition to being a judge, a priest, and a prophet, Samuel was also one of the great "prayer intercessors" in the Old Testament (Psalm 99:6; Jeremiah 15:1). Samuel is included in Hebrews (11:32) as a hero of the faith.

12. (d.) The story of David and Jonathan is usually taught to children, but the intrigues and entanglements of court life are not child's play. 1 Samuel 18–20 records how Jonathan, the technical heir to the throne of Saul, his father, defended David, his father's enemy. King David long remembered his special covenant with Jonathan and extended kindness to his friend's lame son, Mephibosheth. David's lament for the slain Jonathan (and Saul), "How the mighty have fallen," is one of the most uplifting eulogies in Scripture (2 Samuel 1:17–27).

13. (a.) In the context of Lazarus' death, Jesus comforted Martha with the essence and result of salvation. Martha's response was an act of faith. She acknowledged Jesus as the Christ, the Son of God — even before He raised Lazarus from the dead (John 11:21–46).

14. (b.) During Ezekiel's commissioning interview, God told the prophet to eat a book filled with "lamentations, mourning and woe" (Ezekiel 2:9–3:4). Ezekiel obeyed and the "snack" was "sweet as honey" in his mouth. In the New Testament, John was also asked to eat a book. While John's morsel was sweet in his mouth, it was bitter to his stomach (Revelation 10:9–10). The difference between the "meals" may lie in the fact that Ezekiel's prophecies offered eventual redemption, while John's prophecies unleashed final judgment.

15. (a.) The events in the life of Elijah the Tishbite are the stuff of which epics are made. He appeared in 1 Kings 17 without a "past." He raised a widow's dead son. He troubled King Ahab. He challenged 450 prophets of Baal. He feared Jezebel. He was fed by ravens. He was taken to heaven in a fiery whirlwind. He was one of the most mysterious and powerful proph-

ets of the Old Testament. Elijah (Elias) is mentioned thirty times in the New Testament.

16. (d.) The "noble-minded" Bereans daily examined the Scriptures to verify Paul's message (Acts 17:10–12).

17. (b.) Lot, rescued by angels from the destruction of Sodom, fell victim to the wiles of his scheming daughters. Lot's incestuous relationships with the two girls produced Moab, the father of the Moabites, and Ben-ammi, the father of the Ammonites (Genesis 19:30–38). During the Exodus, the Ammonites and the Moabites refused the Israelites safe passage and hospitality. As a result, the Moabites and the Ammonites were excluded from the assembly of the Lord (Deuteronomy 23:3–6).

18. (a.) The wicked Athaliah, the daughter of Ahab and Jezebel, married Jehoram, the son of Jehoshaphat, and produced Ahaziah. When Jehoram and Ahaziah both died, Athaliah set her sights on the throne. In order to rule, she murdered nearly all of her grandchildren, almost wiping out the Davidic line. Only Joash, who was hidden by Jehoiada, escaped (2 Kings 11:1–16; 2 Chronicles 22:10–23:21).

19. (a.) Herod the Great (37–4 B.C.) was the maniacal ruler when Jesus was born. Herod Antipas (4 B.C.–39 A.D.) beheaded John the Baptist and tried Jesus (Mark 6:14–29; Luke 23:7–12). Herod Agrippa I (37–44 A.D.) killed the Apostle James but he himself was later eaten by worms (Acts 12:1–2; 20–23). Herod Agrippa II (50–70 A.D.) tried Paul (Acts 25:13–26:32).

20. (c.) Joseph's sons, Manasseh and Ephraim, were included with the sons of Jacob in the blessing to Joseph (Genesis 48:8–22). Jacob's blessing, contrary to custom, promoted Ephraim, the younger, over Manasseh, the firstborn. This promotion materialized when the kingdom split and the tribe of Ephraim gained superiority over the tribe of Manasseh.

21. (b.) Joab was the overbearing general in David's army who often took matters into his own hands (2 Samuel 3:6–30; 18:5–14. See also the Amasa passages: 2 Samuel 17:24–26; 18:6–8; 19:13; and 20:9–12.) Joab exhibited little reliance on God. Still this domineering man is mentioned more often in Scripture than Isaac.

22. (c.) Jesus descended from the tribe of Judah; Saul was a Benjamite (1 Samuel 9:16, 21).

23. (a.) Hannah knew God opened and closed wombs. So, it was before God that Hannah pleaded for a child. Her fervent prayer caused Eli to rebuke her for drunkenness (1 Samuel 1:9–18). Her equally fervent thanksgiving (1 Samuel 2:1–10) magnified the message of Psalm 9:10: "those who know Thy name will put their trust in Thee."

24. (c.) Abraham declared that Moses and the prophets were capable of convincing the rich man's brothers of eternal judgment (Luke 16:28–31). Abraham's comment anticipated the later reaction of the Jews to Jesus (Acts 7).

25. (a.) King Ahab, who dauntlessly expanded the borders of the Northern Kingdom of Israel against all manner of enemies, could not control his queen (1 Kings 16:28–22:40). Ahab, a study in wickedness, established Baal worship in Samaria, provoked the Lord, disregarded the prophets, and coveted Naboth's puny, tribal inheritance.

26. (d.) Jesus cured Bartimaeus of blindness (Matthew 20:29–34; Mark 10:46–52). Scripture records nearly three dozen of Jesus' miracles. What modern "list-makers" exclude is the greatest miracle, salvation, which transforms a corrupt human spirit and makes it suitable for a relationship with God.

27. (a.) Jeshua (Ezra 2:2) or Joshua (Haggai 1:1) was the high priest when the temple was rebuilt. Although the Return period is rarely the subject of a Sunday sermon, it offers several examples of godly men, including Joshua. The high priest is mentioned twenty-eight times in Ezra and Nehemiah, and the first "message" from Haggai was directed to him (Haggai 1:1–15). Joshua is a key figure in the prophecies of Zechariah (3; 6:11–13).

28. (d.) Laban had two daughters: Leah was the elder, Rachel the younger (Genesis 29:16; 30:1–4, 10). In the strange affairs of the heart (and the customs of Laban), Leah, Rachel, and their handmaidens dominated Jacob's life in Haran. Although Jacob loved Rachel more than Leah, Leah produced six of Jacob's sons: Reuben, Simeon, Levi, Judah, Issachar, and Zebulun. Leah, not Rachel, was buried with Jacob in the cave of Machpelah (Genesis 49:31).

29. (c.) Luke's gospel and the Acts of the Apostles were both written for the instruction of "most excellent Theophilus" (Luke

1:1–4; Acts 1:1–2). Luke's use of the phrase "most excellent" in addressing the Roman officials, Felix and Festus (Acts 23:26; 26:25), have led scholars to believe that Theophilus was part of Rome's bureaucracy. Luke 1:4 clearly identifies Theophilus as someone with whom the writer had shared the basic truths of the gospel.

30. (a.) Miriam, Naaman, Gehazi, and Uzziah all suffered from leprosy, but Miriam's affliction was the direct result of her murmuring against Moses (Numbers 12:1–15). God used Miriam the leader, and God punished Miriam the sinner.

31. (b.) Absalom's forces had David on the run (2 Samuel 15:7 – 18:33). Much is made about David's role as a father and Absalom's role as a son, but Absalom's treason was a consequence of David's sin with Bathsheba (2 Samuel 12:7–12).

32. (c.) The very wealthy Joseph of Arimathea was a dissenting member of the Sanhedrin at the time of the Crucifixion (Luke 23:50–51). Joseph courageously sought Pilate's permission to remove Jesus' body from the Cross and to bury Him in his own tomb (Mark 15:43–46). Joseph's actions fulfilled the prophecy of Isaiah 53:9: "Yet He was with a rich man in His death." All gospel writers take note of Joseph of Arimathea.

33. (c.) God granted Elisha's request. His ministry was kinder, gentler, and more redemptive than that of his predecessor, Elijah. Elisha multiplied a widow's oil, purified a poisonous stew, healed Naaman of leprosy, and opened his servant's eyes to see the protection of God. Most of Elisha's ministry is recorded in 2 Kings 2 – 8.

34. (b.) "Do not be hasty in word or impulsive in thought to bring up a matter in the presence of God" (Ecclesiastes 5:2). Unfortunately, Jephthah, the judge, did not follow Solomon's advice. Jephthah's vow (Judges 11:30–40) was not in keeping with the spirit of the law. Furthermore, Jephthah was evidently ignorant of Leviticus 27:2–8, which made provision for "difficult vows."

35. (a.) The story of Ananias and Sapphira (Acts 5:3) stands in sharp contrast to the characteristically generous spirit of the early church (Acts 4:32–37). Peter's leadership role in the church is clearly seen as he confronts Ananias and his wife.

36. (b.) No doubt Methuselah lived near Noah, his famous grandson, and was probably one of the few people who encouraged Noah as he built the ark. Methuselah was 369 years old when Noah was born (Genesis 5:21–32). Since the Flood occurred when Noah was 600, Methuselah died at age 969 shortly before the Flood.

37. (a.) Priscilla and Aquila instructed Apollos in Ephesus. As a result, Apollos later encouraged the believers in Achaia. Apollos' strength lay in his knowledge of the Scriptures and his ability to refute the Jews' claims against the Messiah (Acts 18:24–28).

38. (c.) Rabshakeh, a military officer in Sennacherib's army, made the inhabitants of Jerusalem quake with his threats. Hezekiah did not quake for long, however. The king wisely laid Rabshakeh's warnings before the Lord. The Lord spared Jerusalem and wiped out the Assyrian army as well (2 Kings 18:17–19:37).

39. (d.) Esther, the Persian/Jewish queen, instituted Purim to commemorate the redemption of the Jews from slaughter (Esther 9:20–32). A key figure in the fast-moving tale is Mordecai, Esther's godly uncle and guardian.

40. (b.) Abner, Saul's cousin, was also his general (1 Samuel 14:50). A man of military skill and understanding, Abner was totally loyal to Saul. After the king's death, Abner placed Saul's only surviving son, Ish-bosheth on the throne. Ish-bosheth's unfounded accusations infuriated Abner who then used his influence to consolidate the crown for David. King David publicly mourned Abner's death by the hand of Joab (2 Samuel 3:31–39).

41. (a.) Mary of Bethany, the long-time friend of Jesus, lovingly anointed Him at a dinner held six days before the Crucifixion. Martha and a healthy Lazarus were in attendance (John 12:1–8).

42. (d.) As chief of operations, Bezalel transformed the blueprints given to Moses into the tabernacle (Exodus 25:40). Bezalel was responsible for the metal, wood, and stone work in the tabernacle (Exodus 31:2–5). Oholiab was the chief "textile" engineer (Exodus 35:30–35).

43. (c.) Annas was the high priest who took part in the trials. Appointed in 6 A.D., Annas served until 15 A.D., when he

was removed by the Romans and replaced with Caiaphas. The Jews considered Annas the high priest of record and deferred to him. Luke lists Annas first when dating the ministry of John the Baptist (3:2). More importantly, the prisoner, Jesus, was taken to Annas before He was taken to Caiaphas (John 18:13, 24). In Acts 4:6 Luke directly calls him, "Annas the high priest."

44. (d.) Both David and Absalom respected Ahithophel (2 Samuel 16:23), one of David's trusted advisors (2 Samuel 15:12). Ahithophel backed Absalom's overthrow and advised the usurper to violate his father's concubines (2 Samuel 16:20–23). When Ahithophel's later advice was thwarted, he committed suicide (2 Samuel 17:15–23). Scripture reveals that Ahithophel the Gilonite had a son named Eliam (2 Samuel 23:34). In 2 Samuel 11:3 Bathsheba is identified as the daughter of Eliam, which would make David's wife the granddaughter of Ahithophel. Thus, Nathan's prophecy from God, "I will raise up evil against you from your own household," more than came true in David's case (2 Samuel 12:11).

45. (a.) In Joppa, Peter raised Dorcas from the dead (Acts 9:36–42). Peter's other miracles centered on healing: a lame man, multitudes in Jerusalem, and Aeneas (Acts 3:2–8; 5:12–15; 9:32–35). In every case, the miracles led to a number of other conversions.

46. (d.) Rachel died giving birth to Benjamin, Jacob's youngest son. In Egypt, Joseph used Jacob's love for Benjamin to bring about the reconciliation with his brothers (Genesis 30:1–24; 35:16–18; 42–46; 50:12–21).

47. (c.) Eve, one of the most pivotal females in Scripture, is called Adam's "wife" before the serpent invaded Eden (Genesis 2:24–25). This lady, whose apple upset humanity's perfect cart, is only mentioned by name four times in all the Bible: twice in Genesis (3:20; 4:1) and twice in Paul's epistles (2 Corinthians 11:3; 1 Timothy 2:13).

48. (b.) The God of Israel often used nonbelievers for His own good purposes. Numbers 22–24 recounts the story of Balaam, the pagan prophet whose life was spared because his donkey collapsed under him. God preserved Balaam to utter eloquent and far-sighted prophecies about Israel. New Testa-

ment references to Balaam are included as warnings (2 Peter 2:16, Jude 11, and Revelation 2:14).

49. (c.) Uzzah's death reflected on David, who, as king, should have written a copy of the law in his own hand (Deuteronomy 17:18). Then, David would have known that the ark of God was designed to be carried, not transported on a cart (Exodus 25:14; Numbers 4:15). Three months after Uzzah's death, "bearers" moved the ark to Jerusalem under David's direction (2 Samuel 6:13).

50. (d.) John wrote the stern warning (Revelation 22:18–19). While the prophecy applies to the book of Revelation, the concept, seen elsewhere in Scripture, is a solemn, closing reminder (Deuteronomy 4:2; 12:32; Proverbs 30:5–6).

PART TWO

THE POSTBIBLICAL PERIOD

NINE

DOCTRINE

THERE WAS PROBABLY NOT MUCH FANFARE when a stocky monk nailed a Latin document to the door of Castle Church on October 31, 1517. Scholars had traditionally pounded messages on the doors of churches to stir up academic debate. But, Martin Luther's carefully worded "theses" weren't just for the learned; his manifesto attacked a widespread practice of the day.

What prompted Luther's action?

Indulgence! Indulgence is not a term most of us use unless we've eaten a sumptuous dinner or a gooey dessert. In the Middle Ages, however, indulgence was a way of life. The popes of Rome had earlier decreed that the penalty for sin could be lessened or pardoned if the sinner paid a fee. The pardon was called an indulgence.

The practice of buying and selling indulgences, traditionally called "the holy trade," was based on the theory that Christ and by-gone saints had credited more good works to their account than was necessary for their own salvation. There were, in fact, enough good works that the pope could transfer the superfluous "credits" to other accounts.

What kinds of sin did indulgences pardon?

The use of butter, for one.

In Rome and throughout the Mediterranean region, olive oil was king. Butter was scarce and hard to keep in the warm climate. Butter was also one of the foods banned during Lent.

In southern Europe, the butter ban was no problem. In northern climates, where butter was widely used, the ban annoyed the faithful. To make matters worse, vendors from the south annually trekked to central and northern Europe peddling a substitute — olive oil. The oil mongers outraged the butter users.

To quiet the uproar, the Church sold indulgences which permitted the use of butter in exchange for the fee. Luther's reaction to the indulgences was understandable: "For at Rome they themselves laugh at the fasts, making us foreigners eat the oil with which they would not grease their shoes, and afterwards selling us liberty [an indulgence] to eat butter."

At the heart of Luther's frustrations was a prevalent teaching which conflicted with Scripture. To the monk, teaching meant doctrine and sound doctrine was historically important. Jesus distinguished between teachers of sound doctrine and mere glory-seekers (John 7:16–18). John warned against encouraging false teachers (2 John 10). Paul urged Timothy: "instruct certain men not to teach strange doctrines" (1 Timothy 1:3). Luther embraced doctrine, plunged into Scriptures, and his conclusions refocused Christianity.

Since certain doctrines often spark debate, we moderns tend to shy away from doctrine altogether. As a result, we ignore a broad set of Christian teachings that are fundamental to our faith. These doctrines are biblically sound, basically noncontroversial, and help us organize our beliefs about foundational issues, such as God, sin, heaven, and hell. Because Christianity prompts a believer to live out the principles of his faith, the Christian's beliefs are important. As Dietrich Bonhoeffer concludes: "life is an extension of what you truly believe."

As we examine our beliefs, questions arise. Who is Satan? What does the Holy Spirit do? How can I be "born again"? These practical questions fall under the umbrella of doctrine. Although we will not address all Bible doctrines in the section that follows, we will look at several basic concepts covered by eight major doctrines: the Bible, God, Christ, the Holy Spirit, angels, man, salvation, and future things.

Questions

1. Doctrine is

    a. a list of rules.

b. a collection of thoughts from Reformation writers.

c. the basic teachings about the major subjects of the Bible.

d. a summary of the apostles' teachings.

2. To those who believe in Jesus Christ as Lord and Savior, God offers forgiveness of sin and

a. material rewards on earth.

b. good health.

c. freedom from temptation.

d. eternal life with Him.

3. The systematic study of God is called

a. theophany.

b. theology.

c. theocracy.

d. theosophy.

4. In the Bible the personality of the Holy Spirit is most clearly developed in the

a. Old Testament historical books.

b. the poetical books.

c. the prophetical books.

d. the New Testament.

5. The evidence that supports the resurrection of Jesus is

a. the empty, opened tomb.

b. Jesus' predictions about His resurrection.

c. Jesus' postresurrection appearances.

d. all of the above.

6. The study of future or last things is called

a. eschatology.

b. ecclesiology.

c. soteriology.

d. doxology.

7. The angel who aspired to be like the "Most High" was

    a. Michael.
    b. Lucifer.
    c. Gabriel.
    d. the angel of the Lord.

8. According to Scripture, human beings originated in the following way:

    a. God created the first man and woman.
    b. Scripture does not mention humanity's origin.
    c. Human beings resulted from natural law set in motion at Creation.
    d. Humanity was part of the fallen angels thrown out of heaven.

9. The "attributes of God" are

    a. physical features.
    b. God's personal characteristics.
    c. a summary of His covenants.
    d. the things God detests.

10. The concepts of revelation, inspiration, illumination, and interpretation are associated with the doctrine of

    a. future things.
    b. salvation.
    c. humankind.
    d. the Bible.

11. The verse which explicitly affirms the deity of Jesus Christ is

    a. "Jesus wept."

    b. "In the beginning was the Word, and the Word was with God, and the Word was God. He was in the beginning with God."

c. "And the Child continued to grow and become strong, increasing in wisdom; and the grace of God was upon Him."

d. all of the above.

12. The sin of Adam was imputed to his offspring. The word *imputed* means

a. to forgive totally.
b. to bankrupt.
c. to reckon or charge something against one's account.
d. to rescue.

13. Angels are

a. ministering spirits.
b. spirit beings created before man.
c. an unknown number of heavenly hosts.
d. all of the above.

14. Jesus said, "I will ask the Father, and He will give you another Helper." The Helper is

a. the Holy Spirit.
b. the church.
c. angels.
d. John the Baptist.

15. The best description of salvation

a. a bilateral (conditional) covenant.
b. a gift.
c. a human right.
d. all of the above.

16. The Great White Throne Judgment is

a. God's judgment on sin at Calvary.
b. God's judgment on Israel by the Assyrians.
c. God's final judgment on the wicked.
d. God's judgment on Judah by the Babylonians.

17. According to Romans 1:20, testimony to God's existence comes via

    a. the prophets.
    b. Creation.
    c. demons.
    d. national fables and myths.

18. The title is *not* associated with Satan is

    a. seraph.
    b. devil.
    c. prince and god of this world.
    d. old serpent.

19. A ministry of the Holy Spirit is

    a. glorifying Jesus.
    b. bringing peace to the world.
    c. destroying the kingdom of Satan.
    d. restoring the kingdom to Israel.

20. To bear sin and to take it away is called

    a. repentance.
    b. atonement.
    c. adoption.
    d. conviction.

21. The second coming of Christ means

    a. Jesus' postresurrection appearances in Jerusalem.
    b. Jesus' meeting with John on the island of Patmos.
    c. Jesus' future return to establish His earthly kingdom.
    d. the Holy Spirit's descent at Pentecost.

22. The word that describes man's inability to make himself acceptable to God is

    a. contrition.
    b. communication.
    c. predestination.
    d. depravity.

23. The New Testament title that emphasizes Jesus' humanity is

    a. Immanuel.
    b. Son of the Most High.
    c. Son of Man.
    d. Lamb of God.

24. Revelation is

    a. the process by which men seek to understand truth.
    b. God's unveiling of truth to man.
    c. the accurate recording of God's truth.
    d. the ministry of the Holy Spirit whereby He enlightens the human mind to understand spiritual truth.

25. Demons are disembodied spirits. In the Gospels they

    a. entered people and animals, altering their ability to function normally.
    b. caused famines.
    c. caused windstorms.
    d. do not appear.

26. The "gifts" of the Holy Spirit are

    a. rewards given to leaders.
    b. spiritual abilities given to all believers to build up the church.
    c. three personal requests granted to all believers.
    d. crowns, such as the crown of life.

27. The _____ of the Old Testament were substitutionary in nature; they accomplished for the Israelite what he could not do for himself.

    a. Sacrifices
    b. Feast days
    c. Tithes
    d. Taxes

28. At the judgment seat of Christ
    a. the antichrist and false prophet are judged.
    b. God judges Gentile nations for their treatment of Israel.
    c. the fallen angels are judged.
    d. the believer accounts for his conduct in life.

29. Interpretation is
    a. the process by which men seek to understand truth.
    b. God's unveiling of truth to man.
    c. the accurate recording of God's truth.
    d. the ministry of the Holy Spirit whereby He enlightens the human mind to understand spiritual truth.

30. The significance of Jesus' death on the cross was
    a. Jesus' death ended the Roman occupation of Palestine.
    b. Jesus' death made possible man's salvation from sin.
    c. Jesus' martyrdom inspired courage in others.
    d. all of the above.

31. When a Christian dies, his body returns to dust and his spirit
    a. returns to dust also.
    b. wanders aimlessly until judgment.
    c. returns to God.
    d. ceases to exist.

32. The names *Adonai, Elohim,* and *Jehovah* reveal the nature of
    a. the Trinity.
    b. God the Father.
    c. Jesus.
    d. the Holy Spirit.

33. The name of the wicked world ruler whose mark is 666 is
    a. Apollyon.
    b. Magog.
    c. the beast.
    d. Maher-shalal-hash-baz.

34. The work of the Holy Spirit which pricks man's conscience about sin and judgment is

    a. the sealing of the Holy Spirit.
    b. regeneration.
    c. baptism.
    d. conviction.

35. Inspiration is

    a. the process by which men seek to understand truth.
    b. God's unveiling of truth to man.
    c. the accurate recording of God's truth.
    d. the ministry of the Holy Spirit whereby He enlightens the human mind to understand spiritual truth.

36. The occurrence at which Jesus laid aside His glory, but not His deity, and became a man is called

    a. the Annunciation.
    b. the Incarnation.
    c. the Transfiguration.
    d. the Crucifixion.

37. The process whereby a believer, through the power of the Holy Spirit, sets himself apart from sinful practices and purifies himself for service to God is called

    a. sanctification.
    b. conviction.
    c. regeneration.
    d. repentance.

38. The verse that affirms the concept of the Trinity is

    a. "And this is the promise which He Himself made to us: eternal life."

    b. "And we know that God causes all things to work together for good to those who love God, to those who are called according to His purpose."

    c. "The grace of the Lord Jesus Christ, and the love of God, and the fellowship of the Holy Spirit, be with you all."

    d. "For I am confident of this very thing, that He who began a good work in you will perfect it until the day of Christ Jesus."

39. According to Revelation, Satan's ultimate fate will be that he

    a. dies at Armageddon.
    b. is cast into the Lake of Fire.
    c. seeks God's forgiveness.
    d. is killed by the two witnesses.

40. Grace is

    a. a gift from God which extends mercy to sinners.
    b. a reasoned trust in God.
    c. deliberately and intelligently willing the best for others.
    d. none of the above.

41. In connection with the Bible, the term *exegesis* is

    a. the name of the original Bible manuscripts.
    b. the study of Hebrew, Greek, and Aramaic.
    c. the study of future things.
    d. a method of studying a Bible passage.

42. God's ability to apply knowledge so that the best possible purposes are realized by the best possible means is called

    a. righteousness.
    b. wisdom.
    c. mercy.
    d. omnificence.

43. One can determine "sound doctrine" by understanding that

    a. if people agree on a teaching, the teaching is "sound doctrine."

b. sound doctrine develops as people practice their faith.

c. sound doctrine never conflicts with Scripture.

d. sound doctrine makes people tolerant of all beliefs.

44. A believer is sealed by the Holy Spirit

    a. when the believer has matured in faith.

    b. immediately before death.

    c. at salvation.

    d. when a believer becomes a church leader.

45. On earth, the portion of person's nature that is "born again" is

    a. the body.

    b. the spirit.

    c. the body and spirit.

    d. it is not possible to be born again.

46. Illumination is

    a. the process by which men seek to understand truth.

    b. God's unveiling of truth to man.

    c. the accurate recording of God's truth.

    d. the ministry of the Holy Spirit whereby He enlightens the human mind to understand spiritual truth.

47. To say God is omnipotent means that

    a. God is unlimited by space.

    b. God's knowledge of past, present, and future is complete and immediate.

    c. God can neither sin or tolerate sin.

    d. God has the power and freedom to do everything consistent with His nature.

48. The doctrinal term given to a body of false teaching is

    a. heresy.

    b. fundamentalism.

    c. evangelicalism.

    d. paradox.

49. "The view that when all the facts become known, they will demonstrate that the Bible in its original autographs [writings] and correctly interpreted is entirely true and never false in all it affirms." This is a definition of

    a. apostolic succession.
    b. propitiation.
    c. inerrancy.
    d. secular humanism.

50. In the study of "future things," the *last* event will be

    a. the "new heavens and the new earth" are created.
    b. the Times of the Gentiles end.
    c. Israel and Judah are reunited.
    d. The Great Tribulation takes place.

Answers

1. (c.) The doctrines of the church are the basic teachings about the major subjects of the Bible.

2. (d.) Salvation includes eternal life with God. A Biblical principal often overlooked is that every man will spend eternity somewhere: the wicked in eternal punishment (Matthew 25:46); the righteous in eternal reward (Romans 6:22; Titus 1:2). Even though Scripture does not contain expanded descriptions of eternal life, there are verses which indicate there will be relationship and activity, not mindless existence. In John 17:3, Jesus says: "And this is eternal life, that they may know Thee, the only true God and Jesus Christ whom Thou hast sent." Revelation 22:5 notes that "they [the bond-servants of God] shall reign forever."

3. (b.) Theology is the systematic study of God. Theology looks at the existence, the person, the names, the attributes, and the works of God and includes the study of the Trinity. The word *theology* also refers to the general study of religious truth and is used interchangeably with the term *doctrine*.

4. (d.) The New Testament presents the personality of the Holy Spirit, while the Old Testament provides only vignettes of His Person and work. Before Pentecost, the Holy Spirit partici-

pated in Creation (Genesis 1:2), guided Moses and the seventy elders (Numbers 11:17–30), empowered the judges (Judges 3:10; 6:34; 15:14–15), prepared David to reign and to write (1 Samuel 16:13–18; Matthew 22:43), and inspired the words of all the prophets (2 Peter 1:21).

Because the Holy Spirit does not "speak for Himself" in Scripture, there is a tendency to think of Him as "lacking personality." However, in the Gospels, Jesus focuses sharply on the individuality of the Holy Spirit, who convicts or rebukes (John 16:8), teaches (John 14:26), and can be blasphemed (Matthew 12:31). The epistle writers reveal more about His nuturing care. The Holy Spirit intercedes for believers during prayer (Romans 8:26), appoints men to ministries (Acts 13:2), and influences lifestyles (Galatians 5:16–26). Moreover, in Galatians 4:6 the Holy Spirit speaks!

5. (d.) The empty tomb, Jesus' personal predictions, and His various postresurrection appearances are three pieces of evidence verifying His resurrection. Add to those facts, the eyewitness accounts of the soldiers guarding the tomb (Matthew 28:4), the message of the angel (Matthew 28:2–5), the reports of the women (Mark 16:1–10), the rumpled linen burial wrappings (Luke 24:12), and the evidence becomes overwhelming. In addition, there were a number of people who saw Jesus after His ascension, among them Stephen (Acts 7:55–56), Ananias (Acts 9:3–16), Paul (Acts 22:17–18; 1 Corinthians 15:5–8), and John (Revelation 1:12–20).

6. (a.) The study of future things is called eschatology. Eschatology examines the roles of Israel, the church, and the Gentile nations as history draws to a close and explores general topics, such as the return of Christ, death, heaven and hell, judgment, and the re-creation of the world.

7. (b.) Lucifer, also called the "son of the dawn" (NASB, NIV), aspired to be like the "Most High" (Isaiah 14:12–15). We learn more about this angel from Ezekiel 28:12b–19, where he is compared to the king of Tyre. Ezekiel states that Lucifer was a "covering cherub." That designation may not mean much to us, but it did to Ezekiel, who actually saw the cherubim (Ezekiel 10:1–14): the angels in God's "inner circle." As a result of his sin, Lucifer was cast from the "mountain of God," although he

maintained access to other heavenly places (Job 1:6–12; 2:1–7; Zechariah 3:1–2).

8. (a.) Scripture states: "And God created man in His own image, in the image of God He created him; male and female He created them" (Genesis 1:27). The creation of man was a direct act of God.

9. (b.) The attributes of God are His personal characteristics. In theology there are two kinds of attributes: communicable and incommunicable. Communicable attributes are those which God shares with humanity, such as love, mercy, justice, and wisdom. Incommunicable attributes, such as omnipresence, omniscience, and omnipotence, belong to God alone.

10. (d.) The concepts of revelation, inspiration, illumination, and interpretation, when studied together, explain the authority of the Bible.

11. (b.) Deity means the "essential nature" of God. The deity of Jesus was the primary thrust of the gospel of John where we are told: "In the beginning was the Word, and the Word was with God, and the Word was God" (John 1:1).

12. (c.) Imputed means to "reckon or charge against" one's account. There are two reasons why imputation is an important concept in the study of sin and salvation. First, the sin of Adam was imputed to his descendants (Romans 5:12–14). Second, the righteousness of God is imputed to those who believe in Jesus Christ (2 Corinthians 5:21).

13. (d.) Angels are ministering spirits who were created before humanity (Luke 2:13; Hebrews 1:14; Job 38:4–7). Their normal duties range from warning God's people (Matthew 2:13) to issuing orders (Daniel 4:13–17) to announcing special births (Luke 1:11–20).

14. (a.) The "Helper" of John 14:16 is the Holy Spirit (14:26), who is also called the "Comforter" and "Advocate." The names come from the Greek word *parakletos*, meaning "a legal assistant, one called to plead a case for someone else." The Greek word translated "another" is significant because it really means "another of the same kind." Christ promised the disciples a "Helper" just like Himself.

15. (b.) Salvation by grace through faith in Christ is purely and simply a gift from God (Ephesians 2:8–9).

16. (c.) The Great White Throne Judgment is the last judgment in Scripture and occurs after Satan is eternally damned (Revelation 20:7-15). This judgment is only for the wicked.

17. (b.) According to Romans 1:20, Creation testifies to the existence of God: "For since the creation of the world His invisible attributes, His eternal power and divine nature, have been clearly seen, being understood through what has been made." The existence of God is a major area of theological study. Scripture in no way attempts to prove God's existence; Scripture assumes "God is." Man, however, offers "arguments" concerning the existence of God. The cosmological argument states that every effect must have a cause. The universe is the effect, therefore, there must be a cause [God]. The teleological argument says that the order in the universe leads one to assume a master designer [God]. The ontological argument states that God exists because man can imagine a perfect being, and, therefore, a perfect being [God] must exist.

18. (a.) *Seraph*, a name which means "fiery" or "burning one," describes a particular kind of worshiping angel. All we know about seraphim is found in Isaiah 6:1-7.

19. (a.) John 14-16 teaches that the Holy Spirit glorifies Christ: "the Spirit of truth . . . . He will bear witness of Me" (John 15:26). "He [the Holy Spirit] shall glorify Me; for He shall take of Mine, and shall disclose it to you" (John 16:14).

20. (b.) To bear sin and to take it away is called atonement. Atonement is the work of Jesus Christ which completely removes the penalty for past, present, or future sin. Christ's death on the Cross is the satisfaction or propitiation paid to God for all sin (1 John 2:2).

21. (c.) The second coming of Christ, mentioned over 300 times in the New Testament alone, is an eschatological term used to describe Jesus' return to earth to establish His kingdom. Like the First Coming, Scripture does not pinpoint the time but offers general guidelines. The Second Coming will be public and visible (Zechariah 14:4), unexpected (Matthew 24:32-51), and a time of accounting and judgment on earth (Luke 19:11-27; Roman 2:5-11).

22. (d.) Depravity describes man's inability to make himself acceptable to God. Depravity means "in a state of corruption."

While man can do good at times, he does not have the capability to avoid evil. A Holy God cannot fellowship with a sinful, corrupted being. Because of his flawed nature, man can never make himself acceptable to God.

23. (c.) The title *Son of Man* identifies Christ with the nature, qualities, and frailties of man. The title is the theme of Luke's gospel and stresses both the humanity of Jesus and the desperate need of the humans He came to save.

24. (b.) Revelation is God's unveiling of truth to man. Scripture teaches that revelation came through three distinct avenues: Creation (Romans 1:20), Jesus Christ (Hebrews 1:1–3a), and the written word of God (Psalms 12:6; 19:7–11; 119:89–93,105; Proverbs 30:5–6; Isaiah 55:10–11).

25. (a.) In the New Testament, demons, sometimes called "unclean spirits," entered a person or animal and altered their ability to function normally (Matthew 9:32–33; Mark 5:1–14; 16:9). The origin of demons is not known. Some scholars theorize that they were part of the "fallen angels" (2 Peter 2:4); others identify demons as the offspring of angels and antediluvian women (Jude 6; Genesis 6:2). The demons recognized Jesus and had profound fear of Him (Mark 1:23–28).

26. (b.) The "gifts" of the Holy Spirit were special abilities given to all believers to strengthen the church; they were not for personal glory (Romans 12:6–8; 1 Corinthians 12). The gifts, properly used, encouraged believers (1 Corinthians 12:8) and attracted nonbelievers (1 Corinthians 14:22).

27. (a.) The sacrifices of the Old Testament were substitutionary. The Israelites understood that blood atoned for sin. The Jew chose an unblemished animal to offer in place of himself. In a similar fashion, Jesus, the unblemished Lamb of God, offered Himself in place of the sinners with whom He identified.

28. (d.) At the judgment seat of Christ, the believer accounts for the conduct of his life (2 Corinthians 5:10; Ephesians 6:7–8). This is not a time of judgment for sin. Sin was judged at Calvary, and there is now no condemnation for those who are in Christ (Romans 8:1). The judgment seat of Christ is exclusively a time of evaluation for service.

29. (a.) Interpretation is the process by which men seek to understand truth. The Bible reveals truth, but Scripture makes it clear that man must avail himself of that truth: "Be diligent to present yourself approved to God as a workman who does not need to be ashamed, handling accurately the word of truth" (2 Timothy 2:15). The study of interpretation is called hermeneutics, which looks at scriptural verses in light of the total message of the Bible, the type of literature (prophetical, epistolary, etc.), the intended audience, the context, and other related Bible passages.

30. (b.) Jesus' death made possible man's salvation from sin. Christ purchased salvation for a price (1 Corinthians 6:20) and that price removed Christians from the authority and penalty of the law (Galatians 4:4–5).

31. (c.) Man's basic nature is composed of body and spirit. At death, man's body returns to dust (Genesis 3:19), but the Christian's spirit will go to be with God (2 Corinthians 5:8).

32. (b.) *Adonai, Elohim,* and *Jehovah* are among the names that reveal the nature of God. *Adonai* means "Lord," a name which reveals the relationship of God to his creatures. When Isaiah saw the Lord (Isaiah 6:1–8), He saw Adonai. *Elohim,* the most commonly used name for God in the Old Testament, reveals God's creativity, omnipotence, and sovereignty. It was first used in Genesis 1:1. *Jehovah* is the personal name of God, the Supreme Being who is totally self-existent and who embodies holiness, righteousness, and love.

33. (c.) The first beast mentioned in Revelation 13 exercises great political authority and is worshiped by all who have not accepted Jesus Christ as Savior. The number 666 is associated with the name of this wicked world ruler.

34. (d.) Conviction is the work of the Holy Spirit which rebukes the world in general and man in particular about sin, righteousness, and judgment (John 16:8). During the conviction process, man is sensitized to spiritual things.

35. (c.) Inspiration is the accurate recording of God's truth. In spite of the fact that human authors penned the words of the Bible, believers have God's assurance that "All Scripture is inspired by God and profitable for teaching, for reproof, for correction, for training in righteousness; that the man of God

may be adequate, equipped for every good work" (2 Timothy 3:16–17). Since Biblical inspiration is supernatural, man has developed theories to explain the phenomenon. Historically, the church has held to the "verbal, plenary inspiration" of the Bible. This means that the Holy Spirit so superintended the choice of words that God's full (not partial) inspiration was recorded.

36. (b.) At the Incarnation Jesus laid aside His glory, but not His deity, and became a man (John 1:14; Philippians 2:5–11; 1 Timothy 3:16). His co-existent natures are reflected in the frequently used titles Son of Man and Son of God. As the Son of Man, Jesus fulfilled the Davidic covenant (Luke 1:31–33), provided the sacrifice for sin (Hebrews 10:1–10), and became a faithful and merciful high priest (Hebrews 2:16–18). As the Son of God, He personally revealed what God the Father is like (John 14:9–11).

37. (a.) Sanctification belongs to a trio of concepts—justification, regeneration, and sanctification—in the doctrine of salvation. Justification pronounces the believer righteous before God (Romans 5:1–2); regeneration identifies him as a child of God (John 3:1–6); and sanctification sets him apart from sinful practices for service to God (Romans 12:1–2; 1 Peter 3:15).

38. (c.) The word *Trinity* describes a supernatural fact: God who is one God manifests His essence in three distinct personalities: the Father, the Son, and the Holy Spirit. The Triune nature of God is seen in 2 Corinthians 13:14: "The grace of the Lord Jesus Christ, and the love of God, and the fellowship of the Holy Spirit, be with you all."

39. (b.) If we "peek" at the future in Revelation (20:10), we see that Satan will be cast into the lake of fire along with the beast and the false prophet.

40. (a.) Grace is a gift from God which extends mercy to sinners (2 Corinthians 5:17–20; 8:9; Ephesians 2:8–9). Grace is central to the doctrine of salvation, which is also called soteriology.

41. (d.) Exegesis, a tool of the interpreter, is a method of studying a Bible passage whereby the reader (the exegete) pays close attention to the meaning of original words, the grammar, the surrounding text, and similar passages of teaching. The ex-

egete draws conclusions from the text rather than using the text to verify preconceived ideas.

42. (b.) God's ability to apply knowledge so that the best possible purposes are realized by the best possible means is called wisdom. Wisdom is one attribute of God for which Scripture encourages men to pray (Proverbs 4:7; James 1:5). Paul pointedly warns believers to distinguish between worldly wisdom and godly wisdom (1 Corinthians 1 – 3).

43. (c.) Sound doctrine upholds Scripture and has nothing to do with either human opinion or human experience (1 Timothy 6:3; 2 Timothy 3:16). Adherence to sound doctrine was a touchstone to measure the authenticity of a teacher's message (Ephesians 4:14). The ability to refute false doctrine was one of the signs of spiritual maturity (Titus 1:9).

44. (c.) The sealing by the Holy Spirit is not a question of "spiritual seniority." A believer is sealed at the moment of belief, the point of salvation (Ephesians 1:13–14). The Holy Spirit's indwelling presence is an indication that spiritual adoption into God's family has occurred.

45. (b.) A person's spirit is "born again" at conversion when he accepts Jesus Christ as personal Savior. As Jesus explained to Nicodemus: "That which is born of the flesh is flesh, and that which is born of the Spirit is spirit" (John 3:6). Thus, on earth, a believer dwells in an unredeemed body with a redeemed spirit. In Romans 7:14 – 8:23 Paul describes the existence as a great struggle. The body's redemption awaits Christ's return (1 Corinthians 15:51–57).

46. (d.) Natural man cannot understand spiritual things, but illumination is the ministry of the Holy Spirit which quickens the mind to spiritual truth (1 Corinthains 2:14; John 16:13). Isaiah 28:10 (KJV) describes the process: "For precept must be upon precept, precept upon precept; line upon line, line upon line; here a little, and there a little."

47. (d.) Omnipotence means that God has the power and freedom to do everything consistent with His nature.

48. (a.) Heresy is the denial of a teaching of Scripture and, therefore, a denial of God's revelation. Heresy may contain some elements of truth, but it deviates from the general conclusions of Scripture. The Bible denounces all heresy or false

teaching (Galatians 1:9). Many heresies have focused on the Trinity or the Incarnation.

49. (c.) Inerrancy is "the view that when all the facts become known, they will demonstrate that the Bible in its original autographs [writings] and correctly interpreted is entirely true and never false in all it affirms." This classic statement was issued by the International Conference on Biblical Inerrancy in October 1978.

50. (a.) Doctrinal neuritis occurs whenever anyone attempts to pinpoint the order of "future events." Yet, without sending a theologian off for an aspirin, it is safe to report that the creation of the "new heavens and the new earth" will be among the last events of human history (Isaiah 65:17; Revelation 21).

TEN

CHURCH HISTORY

"Most of the people are dead and who cares today ?"
Some of life's truths unfold in surprising ways.
It was 6:00 A.M. Chicago on Christmas Eve.
There were no visions of sugar plums. We woke instead to a wind chill of minus 72 degrees, a record even for the Windy City.

This was moving day for my frenzied mother, my infirm father, and his sister, my eighty-year-old aunt. The time had come to exchange the three-story homestead for a one-level condo.

God provided two gifts that Christmas Eve: movers with a sense of humor and a rescued box of family photos. The movers' good cheer soothed the unreality of the event. The photos? The photos came later . . .

"The Big Move" passed into history, and, suddenly, it was Christmas. Nothing was traditional. We heard no angels singing sweetly o'er the plain. There was only wind and an urge to arrange the kitchen and unpack more woollies.

Christmas night with the wind howling and boxes stacked like sequoias, I investigated the carton of photos. Beneath yellowing layers of paper lay turn-of-the-century faces. There was my aunt: hair bobbed, chemised, and very young.

"Look, Auntie, what a sophisticated dress you had!"

Auntie shuffled to the table. She lifted her head slightly to focus through the center of her thick glasses and sat down.

"That was Justine's wedding . . . " she recalled, "a couple of years after Teddy Roosevelt died. Nobody liked my hair."

"Who's this?"

"That's Josephine. You know, my sister, Josephine."

Frankly, the only childhood "Josephine" I recalled was "fat Josephine," one whose arms and legs oozed out of the chairs she settled into.

"She's thin," I replied politely. Then something caught my eye. "Wow! Keystone cops!"

Auntie moved closer. "That's your grandfather. He was a police captain in Hawthorne. That man's his deputy; his name was Steinke. The third man's the truant officer."

I grabbed a post-it, noted the information, and stuck it to the back of the photo. "Grandpa was tall." I observed.

"Yes," she laughed, "tall and bony . . . just like me."

She was right.

"Who's this? He looks like . . . well, uh, like an immigrant."

"Oh, him," Auntie glared. "They got him from the Old Country to marry me, but he ran off and eloped with the neighbor girl. He drank. He was no good."

I was forty-two years old and I had never known that. Auntie had never married. I'd never thought much about her "opportunities." I wanted to know more, but it seemed better to move on.

"Look at the chubby baby."

"That's Sophie's boy. He died the next year from scarlet fever."

"What this?" It was a bent, oversized picture, the interior of a church. Coffins and congregation were everywhere.

Auntie just stared.

My father, who had been watching at a distance, joined in. "That was part of the funeral. It was summer, July 1915, just after my birthday. Western Electric was having its company picnic. Everybody was going off for the day on an excursion steamer named the *Eastland*."

"The boat," Auntie recounted, "moved away from the loading area at the Chicago River. Something happened. There were too many people. The boat tilted out, then shifted suddenly and tipped over toward the dock. Those on deck had some chance, but those below were trapped like our sister Frances. She suffocated, died with more than 800 other people—eight feet from shore."

"She was eighteen." My father added. "It was terrible. There were so many dead there weren't enough hearses. We borrowed a horse and wagon to bury her. With all the funerals it took hours to get to the cemetery. We had to stop once and feed the horse."

"Here's her picture. See." Auntie rummaged through the box and held up a photo of a tall, slender, square-faced young woman. The girl reminded me of my niece.

"She looks like you," Auntie quipped.

She did. We went on.

"Whose wedding?"

Auntie adjusted her glasses.

"I don't know. Do you, Frank?"

My father looked hard at the picture, shook his head, and pushed it back. "They're nobody I know."

"They could be cousins." Auntie explained. "We were the youngest in the family. The youngest don't always know what's going on."

In the fading hours on Christmas night we looked unhurriedly through the loose photos. I interrogated; they reminisced.

Slowly, two stacks formed on the table. One stack of pictures was annotated, clipped with dates, places, and foreign-sounding names—Zdrojewski, Dziewrecki, Wiorkowski—spelled to the best of my ability. The other stack, nearly as tall, contained the portraits of "nobodies," people whose exact identities escaped the recognition of both my father and my aunt.

I eyed the "nobodies." There were lots and lots of nobodies. Some looked jovial. Some were somber. Some were fashionable. Some, I hoped, weren't really relations!

"As for man," the thought flashed, "his days are like grass; as a flower of the field, so he flourishes. When the wind has passed over it, it is no more; and its place acknowledges it no longer."

But, the generation *had not yet passed* and still there was no one to acknowledge these "nobodies."

I sat stunned.

Whether "nobodies" or "somebodies," the pictures exposed a truth I could not deny. Mortality ran in my family!

The evidence was stacked before me.

Family histories add dimension to our lives. Personal facts reveal where we were born, how we fit into our family, who influenced our values, and what traumas shaped our lives. Family history is often oral tradition, retold through an "Auntie," an interpreter tied to both past and present. Family interpreters are cultural gardeners, who graft new generations into the old.

Tucked away in our Christian heritage are ancestors who have shaped our spiritual lineage; but Christian history is rarely retold outside a seminary or Bible college. Therefore modern Christians have not been grafted into their spiritual past. We have only a shadowy understanding of the issues and the people who have shaped our faith. For most of us, church history is like idly poking through a carton of old family photos. There are some interesting sights, an occasional familiar face, but most of the people are dead, and who cares today?

Church history is important. Whether we stem from the older Orthodox, Roman Catholic, or Protestant traditions or from the newer Pentecostal faith, history grafts us to our heritage. It reveals where we, as members of a tradition, were born, how we fit into the family, who influenced our values, and what traumas shaped our faith. Church history gives us an understanding of why we believe, pray, and worship the way we do and clarifies the points at which the traditions of the faith diverged.

The next two chapters, "History: The Church" and "Pivotal Post-New Testament People," survey Christianity from 95 A.D. through the present. The former pays close attention to the concepts that developed, while the latter focuses on the trendsetters. The questions are arranged chronologically to provide continuity and context. The answers are designed to help make the "nobodies" of the Christian faith "somebodies" to you.

Questions

1. The "fathers of church history" were
   a. the first monks.

b. influential church leaders who succeeded the apostles.

c. the bishops of Rome.

d. the early Christian martyrs.

2. The "apologists" were

   a. the writers who defended Christianity against pagan attacks.

   b. the writers who countered false teaching within the Church.

   c. the writers who applied contemporary thinking to theology and developed methods for Biblical interpretation.

   d. the writers who kept records of the martyrs.

3. To "form the canon" of the New Testament meant

   a. to translate the Scriptures into the languages of the people.

   b. to interpret Scripture using contemporary Greek philosophy.

   c. to settle the authority of the basic Church documents.

   d. to adapt Scripture to pagan cultures.

4. The "polemicists" were

   a. the writers who defended Christianity against pagan attacks.

   b. the writers who countered false teaching within the Church.

   c. the writers who applied contemporary thinking to theology and developed methods for Biblical interpretation.

   d. the writers who kept records of the martyrs.

5. The word *orthodox* means

   a. conforming to the established doctrines.

   b. a type of early church building.

c. a division of opinion about the doctrines of Scripture.

d. teaching which contradicts Scripture.

6. The Gnostics believed that

a. man was born good, but society corrupted him.

b. divine revelation continued through the exercise of the spiritual gifts.

c. God created the world.

d. salvation came through secret knowledge plus good works and was available to only a few people.

7. By 100 A.D. the pre-eminent church in Christianity was at

a. Jerusalem.
b. Rome.
c. Constantinople.
d. Alexandria.

8. "The blood of martyrs is the seed of the church" is a quotation from

a. Nero.
b. Marcus Aurelius.
c. Tertullian.
d. Diocletian.

9. The "scientific theologians" were

a. writers who defended Christianity against pagan attacks.
b. writers who countered false teaching within the church.
c. writers who applied contemporary thinking to theology and developed methods for Biblical interpretation.
d. writers who kept records of the martyrs.

10. The Roman emperor who tied the church to the state when he made Christianity a legal religion with himself at its head was

a. Diocletian.
b. Constantine.

c. Nero.

d. Constantius.

11. Under Constantine councils were called

a. to settle church disputes.

b. to negotiate territorial disputes.

c. to plan military strategy.

d. to establish trade rights.

12. A basilica was

a. an arena for gladiators.

b. a visit made to the Holy Land.

c. a baptismal candidate.

d. a type of church architecture.

13. After Constantine, the general relationship between Christians and Jews can best be described as

a. the Christians protected the Jews.

b. both the Christians and the Jews prospered.

c. the Jews protected the Christians.

d. the Jews were periodically persecuted.

14. Originally, Lent was a time

a. when baptismal candidates fasted, prayed, and studied.

b. to remember the martyrs.

c. to commemorate Jesus' temptation in the desert.

d. to celebrate Jesus' 40 days as resurrected Lord.

15. Asceticism was

a. inconsistent spiritual devotion.

b. rigorous practice of the faith.

c. a probationary period for converts.

d. a total denial of the faith.

16. Monasticism was

a. emperor rule over the church.

b. voluntary, structured, communal or secluded living.

   c. a heresy that threatened the early church.
   d. blending pagan beliefs with Christianity.

17. The Latin Vulgate was

   a. the bishop of Constantinople.
   b. the governing branch of the church in Rome.
   c. a translation of the Bible.
   d. the barbarian horde which attacked Rome.

18. The word *Christendom* refers to

   a. cities of major religious significance.
   b. geographical areas for foreign missions.
   c. a society in which Christianity dominates.
   d. none of the above.

19. By 700 A.D., the religion which threatened Christianity was

   a. Hinduism.
   b. Judaism.
   c. Buddhism.
   d. Islam.

20. In the Eastern Church, Cyril and Methodius were

   a. missionary/educators.
   b. church musicians.
   c. monk/generals who fought the Turks.
   d. Muslim converts.

21. An icon is

   a. a papal envoy to Constantinople.
   b. an agreement between the pope and a political leader.
   c. holy "images" of Jesus, Mary, and heroes of the faith.
   d. a bishop's headdress.

22. The Crusades were

   a. military ventures sanctioned by the church.
   b. the Muslim buildings established in Spain.
   c. a medieval singing group.

d. monks loyal to the pope.

23. The seven sacraments were officially accepted by the church

    a. in the period 70–100 A.D.
    b. during the reign of Constantine.
    c. in the Middle Ages.
    d. during the Reformation.

24. The Inquisition was

    a. the final examination before confirmation.
    b. the coronation of a pope.
    c. a church court which tried suspected heretics.
    d. the redistricting of local parishes for taxation.

25. The Waldensians were

    a. Catholic missionaries to Japan.
    b. a craft guild which decorated the Sistine Chapel.
    c. lay people who preached from Scripture.
    d. the indulgence sellers of the church.

26. The term Renaissance refers to

    a. an era of renewed interest in learning and individualism.
    b. a spiritual awakening determined to reform church abuses.
    c. a special type of incense.
    d. an important papal encyclical.

27. Belief(s) that characterized the Protestant Reformation was/were

    a. authority of Scripture as the Word of God.
    b. salvation by grace through faith in Jesus Christ.
    c. the priesthood of individual believers.
    d. all of the above.

28. The Reformers were identified as "Protestants" because

    a. Protestant was the name of Luther's parish church.
    b. Luther's supporters were described as "protesters."
    c. John Wycliffe coined the term.
    d. Protestant was the name of Luther's publisher.

29. The five concepts—total depravity, unconditional election, limited atonement, irresistible grace, and perseverance of the saints—are the tenets of

    a. Lutherism.
    b. Calvinism.
    c. Roman Catholicism.
    d. John Hus.

30. "If God spare my life, ere many years pass, I will cause a boy that driveth the plough to know . . . the Scriptures." This statement is associated with the development of

    a. the Sunday school movement.
    b. the translation of the English Bible.
    c. the public school movement.
    d. the establishment of orphanages.

31. The Jesuits (the Society of Jesus) were

    a. Protestant reformers.
    b. Catholic laymen who called for reform in the church.
    c. Catholic monks dedicated to serving the pope.
    d. none of the above.

32. The papal response to the Protestant Reformation was

    a. the Council of Trent.
    b. Vatican II.
    c. the Council of Nicea.
    d. the Council of Constantinople.

33. The city which claimed it was the "third Rome" was

    a. London.
    b. Dublin.

   c. Geneva.

   d. Moscow.

34. The tradition from which the Puritans originated was

   a. Lutheran.

   b. Zwinglian/Calvinist.

   c. Church of England.

   d. Roman Catholic.

35. Deism taught that

   a. God was involved in every facet of society.

   b. God created the world but let it run on natural principles without His further intervention.

   c. church and state together should dictate morals.

   d. the ancient cultures held the key to truth.

36. The Great Awakening was a spiritual revival in

   a. The Eastern Orthodox Church.

   b. North Africa.

   c. the American colonies.

   d. China.

37. Early Methodism was *not* characterized by

   a. assurance of salvation.

   b. creation of societies to nurture converts.

   c. a strong desire to separate from the Church of England.

   d. an appeal to the working masses.

38. The time period of "the Second Great Awakening" was

   a. 1776–1789.

   b. 1789–1870.

   c. 1898–1914.

   d. 1917–1930.

39. Sierra Leone was

   a. a Christian colony for former slaves.

   b. a slum mission in London.

    c. the first school for the deaf.

    d. the first home for the aged.

40. A "mass evangelist" was

    a. an itinerant Catholic priest on the American frontier.

    b. a preacher who evangelized large, urban audiences.

    c. an army chaplain.

    d. a priest who worked in predominantly Protestant areas.

41. The Biblical doctrine that Darwin's theories contradicted was

    a. the ministry of the Holy Spirit.

    b. the deity of Jesus.

    c. the nature of angels.

    d. the origin of man.

42. "Theological liberalism" is associated with the time period of

    a. the Middle Ages.

    b. the Reformation.

    c. the early nineteenth century.

    d. the late-nineteenth and early-twentieth centuries

43. In 1870 Vatican I decreed

    a. the Immaculate Conception of Mary.

    b. papal infallibility on issues of faith and morals.

    c. the direction of twentieth-century Catholic missions.

    d. the creation of U.S. Catholic universities.

44. In the United States, fundamentalism

    a. supported liberal theology.

    b. sought to reconcile the Catholic and Protestant traditions.

    c. opposed liberal theology.

    d. led to the formation of the World Council of Churches.

45. The twentieth-century occurrence(s) which bolstered the credibility of the Bible as a source document for historical evidence was/were

   a. carbon dating of fossils.
   b. the discovery of the Shroud of Turin.
   c. discovery of the Dead Sea Scrolls.
   d. all of the above.

46. Evangelicalism was

   a. belief that God continues His revelation through angels.
   b. an offshoot of the "God-is-dead" movement.
   c. an anti-intellectual, isolationist Christian movement.
   d. none of the above.

47. The geographical focus of "liberation theology" is

   a. the Soviet Union.
   b. Indonesia.
   c. Australia.
   d. Central and South America.

48. The general result of Vatican II was

   a. renewed hostility between Rome and the Eastern Church.
   b. openness to theological issues.
   c. removal of all Catholic universities from papal authority.
   d. Vatican recognition of the state of Israel.

49. Pentecostalism is a tradition of Christianity which

   a. emphasizes a personal experience of the Holy Spirit.
   b. has enjoyed exceptional growth in Latin America and Africa.
   c. has affected mainline Protestantism and Catholicism.
   d. does all of the above.

50. The "electronic church" is the result of

   a. mass evangelism.
   b. foreign missions.

c. archaeology.
d. evangelical scholarship.

Answers

1. (b.) The "fathers" were influential men who succeeded the apostles. Historians frequently divide the fathers into four groups: postapostolic fathers (c. 95–150 A.D.), the apologists (140–200 A.D.), the polemicists (180–225 A.D.), and the scientific theologians (225–430 A.D.). The postapostolic fathers encouraged and instructed the church while the Scriptures were being collected. Among the notable postapostolic fathers are Clement of Rome, Polycarp of Smyrna, and Ignatius of Antioch. (The remaining categories of fathers are treated in answers 2, 4, and 9.)

2. (a.) The apologists, the second group of fathers, defended Christianity against pagan charges, such as atheism (Christians did not worship the emperor or the traditional gods) and cannibalism (a misunderstanding regarding the Lord's Supper). In addition, apologists, like Justin Martyr and Tatian, wrote to win pagans to Christ.

3. (c.) To form the canon of the New Testament means to settle the authority of Scripture. By 100 A.D. all of the New Testament books were written but not collected. Among the first works in the canon were the writings of Paul and the synoptic Gospels. By 397 A.D. the canon of the New Testament was complete with the collection of all twenty-seven books.

4. (b.) While the apologists warded off outside attacks, the polemicists, the third group of fathers, fended off attacks inside the church. Using New Testament Scriptures, polemicists addressed false teaching (e.g., Gnosticism), clarified church positions, and assembled the doctrines which opposed heresy. Among the outstanding polemicists were Irenaeus, Cyprian, and Tertullian.

5. (a.) Orthodox means conforming to the established doctrines. Because early Christians did not have the Scriptures, leaders taught the principles of the faith, frequently using jingles or verses. Eventually, the church established the Rule of

Faith, a loose formula for statements of belief, and the formal creeds which baptismal candidates memorized.

6. (d.) The Gnostics believed that salvation came from a secret knowledge of God plus good works. They taught that the spirit was good and matter was evil, a belief which led to unbiblical conclusions about the divinity and humanity of Jesus. Because of the claims of Gnosticism, the bishops saw themselves as defenders of the faith, and the church developed the tradition of deferring to their wisdom.

7. (b.) After Jerusalem was destroyed (70 A.D.), Rome, the capital of the empire, became the focus for Christianity. Paul wrote the foundational book of Romans to the church at Rome. Tradition holds that Peter and Paul were martyred there, and many of the fathers of church history, such as Polycarp, Justin, Irenaeus, and Origen, lived in the city. The church at Rome promoted its pre-eminence with the concept of apostolic succession.

8. (c.) Tertullian said: "The blood of martyrs is the seed of the church." The faith of martyrs often attracted pagans to Christianity. Persecution was intermittent rather than on-going. The first persecution began after Pentecost when the Jews stoned Stephen. In 64 A.D. Nero set the state policy when he burned some Christians at the stake and threw others to wild animals. Many believers, like Ignatius of Antioch, were funneled into Rome from outlying areas for execution. The most devastating, empire-wide persecution was ordered by Diocletian in 303–305 A.D., just eight years before Christianity became a legal, favored religion.

9. (c.) The "scientific theologians" were the fourth group of church fathers; they applied contemporary thinking to theology and developed methods for Biblical interpretation. Men like Origen, Athanasius, Jerome, Ambrose, Augustine (bishop of Hippo), and John Chrysostom wrote abundantly and their works were held in high esteem.

10. (b.) Constantine's influence on the church cannot be overemphasized. The emperor made Sunday a public holiday and an occasion for worship. He preferred formality and ceremony and introduced court "touches," like burning incense, using candles, and draping the altar. Constantine created the

festival of Christmas, encouraged pilgrimages to the Holy Land, and bequeathed property to the bishop of Rome, thereby reinforcing the idea that the church at Rome was unique.

11. (a.) As the head of all state religions, Constantine felt duty bound to see that the church settled its disputes promptly. In 325 A.D. he convened and presided over the first general church council, the Council of Nicea, which debated the Arian controversy (a heresy which attacked the divinity of Jesus). To underscore Christ's divinity, the council approved the Nicene Creed, but it also set a precedent for emperor intervention in spiritual matters.

12. (d.) A basilica was a building designed to house large numbers of worshipers. The basilica was a rectangular hall with a semicircular opening at one end (called an apse) which separated the clergy from the congregation. The interior was divided by rows of columns into a wider central hall and two or four narrow, parallel aisles. The basilica remained the standard church building in large cities until the medieval cathedrals gained favor.

13. (d.) After Constantine the Jews were periodically persecuted. Sometimes persecution was harassment: paying special taxes or living in ghettos. There were times, such as during the first Crusade, when Jews were slaughtered. In the Middle Ages Jews were special targets of the Inquisition. In the year Columbus discovered the New World, King Ferdinand expelled all Jews from Spain.

14. (a.) Originally Lent was the time when candidates fasted, prayed, and studied before their baptism on Easter.

15. (b.) Asceticism was a rigorous practice of the faith which could require extra prayers and devotions or abstinence from marital relations, sleep, or food. Asceticism was an attempt to maintain purity and high commitment. Although the New Testament did not require ascetic behavior, adherents claimed a precedent in John the Baptist.

16. (b.) Monasticism, an outgrowth of asceticism, was voluntary, structured, communal or secluded living which first appeared in Eastern Christianity. Some monasteries were havens of study. Some became training centers for laymen or clergy, while others were places for treating the sick. Many dedicated

leaders, like Francis of Assisi and Augustine of Hippo, were monastics.

17. (c.) To the early Church "Scripture" meant documents written in Greek, the language of the Septuagint and the apostles. By 150, however, Christians desired a text in Latin, the official language of the empire. In 382 Jerome was commissioned to draft the authorized version of the Latin Scriptures. His text became known as the Vulgate and was the first book which Gutenberg printed a thousand years later.

18. (c.) Christendom refers to a society dominated by Christianity. With the conversion of the Frankish leader, Clovis, in 496, Western Europe became "Christendom," a territory divided into dioceses and parishes, where life from birth to death was regulated by the church.

19. (d.) Islam rose like a searing wind from the desert and scorched its imprint on the Middle East, North Africa, and parts of Europe, once strongholds of Christianity. By 1095 the Muslim threat triggered the Crusades. The "five pillars" of Islam were: (1) belief—"There is no God but Allah, and Mohammed is his prophet"; (2) prayer—five times each day; (3) pilgrimage—to Mecca at least once in life; (4) alms-giving; (5) fasting—during the sacred month of Ramadan.

20. (a.) Around 860 Cyril and Methodius were sent to evangelize the Moravians, descendants of the Slavic people. Cyril prepared an alphabet for their as yet unwritten language, and Eastern Christianity and the Byzantine culture were spread simultaneously. War disrupted the missionaries' efforts and the Moravian Church eventually developed along Roman Catholic lines. Nevertheless, followers of Cyril and Methodius carried their work forward, converting the Bulgarians and the Russians. These missionaries are called the "Apostles to the Slavs."

21. (c.) An icon is an image which some believers in the Eastern Church consider holy and deserving of worship. The Roman Church equated icons with idolatry. This sharp difference of opinion eventually split the church in 1054. The presence of icons in the Christian church bolstered Islam's claim to be the world's only monotheistic religion.

22. (a.) The Crusades were a series of military ventures sanctioned by the medieval Roman church. Although the first

Crusade, organized to defend Constantinople and to liberate the Holy Land from the Muslims, was the most successful, the results were temporary. While the early Crusades sought to contain the "infidels," later Crusades attacked local heretics and individual rulers such as Frederick II.

23. (c.) The Fourth Lateran Council in 1215 authorized seven sacraments: baptism, confirmation, eucharist, penance, extreme unction, ordination, and matrimony. Furthermore, transubstantiation, the belief that the bread and the wine used in the Lord's Supper was transformed into the actual body and blood of Christ, was made doctrine. These concepts, whose origins were not Biblically documented, greatly concerned the later Reformers.

24. (c.) The Inquisition was a medieval church court which tried suspected heretics, many of whom were people wanting to reform or purify the church. Trials were secret. Dominican monks presided as inquisitors, and the accused rarely had legal counsel. Repentant parties paid fines or performed works, but the unrepentant were tortured or executed. The Inquisition, which declined around the fifteenth century, was particularly harsh in Spain.

25. (c.) The Waldensians, founded around 1176, were lay people who preached from Scripture. They began as a movement within the church but their scriptural stance led to their excommunication at the Fourth Lateran Council. The group prospered numerically but became one of the major targets of the Inquisition. Their stand influenced the later Reformers.

26. (a.) The Renaissance man rediscovered the classical languages, particularly, Hebrew and Greek; applauded the invention of cheap paper and the printing press; and questioned authoritarian tradition.

27. (d.) The three great principles of the Protestant Reformation were: the authority of Scripture as the Word of God, salvation by grace through faith in Jesus Christ, and the priesthood of individual believers.

28. (b.) When Charles V restricted Luther's activities in 1529, Luther's supporters "protested" and were labeled "Protestants." The following year, Luther abandoned his attempts to reform the church and issued a statement of belief at Augsburg,

an action which essentially divided Christianity into Orthodox, Roman, and Protestant traditions.

29. (b.) Total depravity, unconditional election, limited atonement, irresistible grace, and perseverance of the saints are the five points of Calvinism, a major branch of Protestantism. These points are easily remembered by using the mnemonic: t-u-l-i-p.

30. (b.) The vision to have "the boy that driveth the plough" actually read the Scriptures in his own language drove men like William Tyndale, Miles Coverdale, and John Rogers to translate the Bible into English.

31. (c.) In addition to vowing poverty, chastity, and obedience, the Jesuits promised unhesitating submission (as unquestioningly "as a corpse") to the pope. The Jesuit order, approved in 1540, pursued foreign missions, established schools, and sought to regain the losses incurred from the Protestant Reformation.

32. (a.) Pope Paul III convened the Council of Trent (1546), one of the most decisive meetings in church history. The council reaffirmed the seven sacraments, placed tradition alongside Scripture as the authority for the church, upheld the value of relics and indulgences, added the Apocrypha to the Latin Vulgate, and increased papal authority. The council's sharp response ruled out a Protestant-Catholic reconciliation.

33. (d.) During the Reformation, the Russian church, aligning itself with the church-state pattern found in Constantinople, claimed that Moscow was the "third Rome." Ivan the Terrible (1533–1584) took the title "czar" (*Caesar* in Russian), thus, tying his reign to the succession of Roman emperors.

34. (c.) The Puritans, prominent in American history, were believers trying to reform the Church of England beyond what had been accomplished by the Reformation. The Puritans became vocal and focal during the reign of Elizabeth who loved religious pomp and circumstance.

35. (b.) Deism taught that God created the world but let it run unsupervised. Deism was the result of eighteenth-century rationalism, the belief that men discovered truth through reason. Deists, such as Benjamin Franklin, George Washington, and Thomas Jefferson, supported religious freedom, endorsed

the separation of church and state, and stressed the dignity of man.

36. (c.) The Great Awakening began in the 1720s in New Jersey with the preaching of Theodore Frelinghuysen, spread in the 1730s to Massachusetts through Jonathan Edwards, and climaxed in the 1740s with George Whitefield. The Awakening led to Indian evangelization, a zeal for higher education, and eventually, political liberation from England.

37. (c.) The counterpart in England of the Great Awakening in America was the Methodist Revival, sometimes called the Evangelical Awakening. Early Methodism assured believers of salvation, provided a society for spiritual growth, and evangelized industrial centers. Methodism found its niche within the Church of England and remained there for fifty years.

38. (b.) The Second Great Awakening began in the aftermath of the Revolutionary War and affected both the United States and Europe. In America the Second Awakening involved outstanding preachers like Charles Finney and D. L Moody, but it was largely a movement of local Presbyterian, Methodist, and Baptist ministers who tamed America's frontier with tent meetings. As a result of the Second Awakening, Christians in the United States embraced foreign missions, created organizations like the American Temperance Union to improve society, and grappled with the issues of slavery.

39. (a.) Sierra Leone was a West African Christian colony for former slaves. The colony was created in 1792 through the efforts of English evangelicals known as the Clapham Sect. The group supported British foreign missions, opposed slavery, and worked to reform the East India Company.

40. (b.) A mass evangelist was a preacher who carried the gospel to large, urban audiences. Mass evangelism had its roots in the Evangelical Awakening when men like Wesley and Whitefield began to evangelize the working classes that had been overlooked by traditional churches. One unique aspect of mass evangelism was its meeting place — usually a field — since there were no large buildings available for "factory crowds."

41. (d.) Darwin's theories contradicted the Biblical concept of the origin of man and rocked the foundations of Christian belief. If human beings were the product of an impersonal evo-

lutionary process, what was the Bible all about? T. H. Huxley's support of Darwin's theory sent scientists, theologians, and politicians scrambling to rethink traditionally held views.

42. (d.) "Theological liberalism" trailed Darwinism in the late ninteenth century. The liberals saw Scripture and doctrine as "evolving" with science, culture, and philosophy. Liberal theologians denied the authority of Scripture, espoused the fatherhood of God and the brotherhood of men, and focused on social reform and political action. Walter Rauschenbusch's "social gospel," Julius Wellhausen's "higher criticism," Albert Schweitzer's "reverence for life," and the modern ecumenical movement are manifestations of liberal thinking.

43. (b.) In response to liberalism, Vatican I anchored Catholics to the belief that the pope was infallible when speaking *ex cathedra* ("from the chair") on issues of faith and morals.

44. (c.) Fundamentalism opposed liberal theology and reaffirmed the infallible, verbal inspiration of Scripture. Fundamentalism took shape in 1909 when several writers, including B.B. Warfield and R.A. Torrey, published a twelve-volume paperback series called *The Fundamentals*. These books set forth the basic doctrines of Christianity, and those who adhered to the beliefs were called fundamentalists.

45. (c.) Before the Dead Sea Scrolls, the oldest Biblical texts dated to the ninth century A.D. The Dead Sea Scrolls yielded copies of the Hebrew Bible dating to the first century B.C. A comparison of the texts confirmed the careful manner with which Biblical manuscripts had been transmitted.

46. (d.) Evangelicalism was a Christian mind-set which rejected the dogmatic, antiintellectual, separatist position of fundamentalism but supported many of its Biblical positions. In belief, evangelicalism emphasized a personal faith in Jesus Christ, affirmed Scriptures as the infallible, inspired Word of God, and upheld the orthodox doctrines of Biblical Christianity. In action, evangelicalism addressed moral issues, such as abortion, drugs, pornography, and ethics, and sought modern solutions based on scriptural principles. In 1979 evangelicals and fundamentalists joined forces in the Moral Majority.

47. (d.) Liberation theology, first espoused by Catholics during the 1960s, focuses its attention on Central and South Amer-

ica. Adherents view sin as man's inhumanity to man rather than rebellion against God. Consequently, liberation theology strives to improve social, economic, and political conditions, using as its authority those portions of Scripture which mention the poor.

48. (b.) The result of Vatican II (1962) was theological openness in the Catholic Church. It was the first council called to evaluate the church's pastoral role rather than settle a dispute. The council promoted the distribution and study of the Bible and encouraged active Catholic cooperation in translation efforts. It sought dialogue with Protestants and representatives of non-Christian religions. Among the changes Catholics witnessed in the church were: the Mass said in native languages (not Latin), increased participation in worship, and congregational singing.

49. (d.) Pentecostalism emphasizes a personal experience of the Holy Spirit. The movement had its roots in a three year revival in the Azusa Street Mission in Los Angeles in 1906. As a result, many denominations were organized: the Church of God in Christ, the Church of God, the Assemblies of God, and the Pentecostal Holiness. In America, Pentecostal (charismatic) influences affected worship and prayer in Protestant and Catholic traditions during the 1960s and 1970s. Internationally, Pentecostalism has enjoyed great numerical success in Latin America and Africa.

50. (a.) The tools of mass evangelism have produced the phenomenon known as the "electronic church." Television and radio have brought the gospel, Bible study, and worship to thousands of people who would not or could not regularly attend a traditional church service. While recent scandals have caused believers to reexamine their loyalties and re-assess their contributions, in responsible hands television remains one of the most powerful tools for communicating the gospel. Ask Billy Graham.

ELEVEN

PIVOTAL POST-NEW TESTAMENT PEOPLE

MOST CHRISTIANS–WHETHER PARTICIPATING IN A STUDY GROUP, listening to a sermon, or playing a Bible quiz game—can easily recognize Biblical characters from the days of Noah through John on the Isle of Patmos. Then they become religious illiterates. Mention Josephus, Boniface, Bernard of Clairvaux—even up to William Booth, William Wilberforce, or Dietrich Bonhoeffer—and they score zero on name recognition.

This is sad because in the last nineteen hundred years church history has been full of thrilling stories about interesting people whose lives have actually affected our own lives. We might think of each one of these as a stone in the gigantic mozaic of "Christianity Today": each one contributes to the totality of effect and leaves a blank space if omitted.

To truly understand our heritage which makes us what we are—like our personal genetic legacy—we must be conversant with the epical sweep of church history and its "Pivotal Post-New Testament People."

Take this quiz and then perhaps you'll be inspired to go to the library and begin brushing up on some of the inspiring, or exciting, or tragic stories of people preceding us, who have contributed to our continuing saga of faith in action.

Questions

1. The statement that is *not* true about Polycarp is that

   a. he was taught by the Apostle John.
   b. he was Bishop of Smyrna until 156 A.D.
   c. he was martyred at age eighty-six.
   d. he witnessed the Crucifixion.

2. The Roman attracted to Christianity because of courageous martyrs was

   a. Justin Martyr.
   b. Marcus Aurelius.
   c. Domitian.
   d. Trajan.

3. A man who worked to offset Gnostic heresy was

   a. Polycarp.
   b. Eusebius.
   c. Irenaeus.
   d. Josephus.

4. The one who first used the term "New Testament," set forth the doctrine of the Trinity, and opposed infant baptism was

   a. Polycarp.
   b. the Apostle John.
   c. Josephus.
   d. Tertullian.

5. The pioneer in systematic theology and Biblical exegesis was

   a. Cyprian.
   b. Origen.
   c. Horace.
   d. Irenaeus.

6. Eusebius, bishop of Caesarea in Palestine, was a(n)

   a. historian.
   b. emperor.
   c. musician.
   d. martyr.

7. Jerome's legacy to Christianity is

   a. religious art from the Eastern church.
   b. the Latin translation of the Bible.
   c. a hymnbook.
   d. a history of his friendship with Constantine.

8. The greatest preacher in the early church was

   a. John Chrysostom.
   b. Jerome.
   c. Ignatius of Antioch.
   d. Athanasius.

9. Augustine, bishop of Hippo, recorded his conversion in

   a. *The Trinity.*
   b. *The City of God.*
   c. *Confessions.*
   d. none of the above

10. Pope Leo the Great was *not* responsible for

    a. assigning special authority to the pope of Rome.
    b. formulating the doctrine that Jesus was fully God and fully man.
    c. persuading Attila the Hun to spare Rome.
    d. starting the Vatican Library.

11. The man who promoted Bible study and evangelism in fifth-century Ireland was

    a. Patrick of Britain.
    b. Sean of Britain.
    c. Thomas of Britain.
    d. George of Britain.

12. The Celtic missionary to Scotland based at Iona was

    a. Finnian of Moville.
    b. Columba.
    c. Finnian of Clonard.
    d. Patrick of Britain.

13. The four "Fathers of Catholicism" are Ambrose, Jerome, Augustine, and

    a. Cyprian of Carthage.
    b. Benedict.
    c. Gregory the Great.
    d. none of the above.

14. *The Ecclesiastical History of the English People* was written by

    a. Augustine.
    b. Patrick.
    c. Boniface.
    d. The Venerable Bede.

15. The "Apostle to the Germans" was

    a. Charles Martel.
    b. Boniface.
    c. Joan of Arc.
    d. Gregory II.

16. Alcuin worked closely with

    a. Charlemagne.
    b. Bede.
    c. Pope Leo III.
    d. Clovis.

17. Bernard of Clairvaux is associated with

    a. stained glass art.
    b. monastic orders for women.
    c. patterns of genetic inheritance.
    d. militant monastic orders.

18. The pilgrims in *The Canterbury Tales* were going to worship at

    a. the shrine of Joan of Arc.
    b. the church at Fatima.
    c. the shrine of Thomas à Becket.
    d. Peter's basilica in Rome.

19. In the twelfth century, at the height of its political power, the church was headed by

    a. Francis of Assisi.
    b. Innocent III.
    c. Dominic de Guzman.
    d. King John of England.

20. The Franciscans religious order was characterized by

    a. poverty.
    b. ministry to Jews.
    c. isolation.
    d. meticulous Bible copying.

21. Thomas Aquinas is remembered as a

    a. pope.
    b. theologian.
    c. missionary.
    d. Bible translator.

22. The belief *not* held by John Wycliffe was

    a. the Bible contains the whole revelation of God.
    b. the papacy is an office instituted by man not God.
    c. transubstantiation was contrary to Scripture.
    d. the pope should be unquestioningly obeyed.

23. John Hus was a

    a. Scandinavian missionary.
    b. musician.
    c. reformer.
    d. leader in the Eastern church.

24. *Imitation of Christ* was written by

    a. Thomas Aquinas.
    b. Erasmus.
    c. Thomas à Kempis.
    d. Catherine of Siena.

25. The "Father of the Protestant Reformation" was

    a. Martin Luther.
    b. John Calvin.
    c. Ulrich Zwingli.
    d. none of the above.

26. The "Third man of the Reformation" was

    a. John Wycliffe.
    b. John Calvin.
    c. Martin Luther.
    d. Ulrich Zwingli.

27. Albrecht Dürer depicted the spirit of the Reformation in his

    a. poetry.
    b. stained glass art.
    c. woodcuts and copper engravings.
    d. music.

28. William Tyndale said: "Lord, open the king of England's eyes," He wanted Henry VIII to see

    a. corruption within the church.
    b. the importance of an English Bible.
    c. the underlying causes of widespread food fights.
    d. the immorality of the King's court.

29. The Jesuits were founded by

    a. Ignatius Loyola.
    b. Pius III.
    c. Francis Xavier.
    d. Matthew Ricci.

30. The Dutch Anabaptist movement was consolidated by

    a. Menno Simons.
    b. Thomas Cranmer.
    c. George Muller.
    d. John Knox.

31. A haven for Protestant refugees in Geneva was provided by

    a. Cardinal Richelieu.
    b. John Calvin.
    c. John Knox.
    d. Cuthbert Tunstall.

32. The Scottish Reformation was led by

    a. Ulrich Zwingli.
    b. George Wishart.
    c. John Knox.
    d. Robert Burns.

33. The *Book of Martyrs* was written by

    a. Miles Coverdale.
    b. Jacob Arminius.
    c. John Foxe.
    d. William Shakespeare.

34. The French scientist, _____, left a legacy of spiritual "notes."

    a. Robert Boyle
    b. Blaise Pascal
    c. Baruch Spinoza
    d. Louis Pasteur

35. *Pilgrim's Progress* was written by

    a. John Bunyan.
    b. John Donne.
    c. John Milton.
    d. John Owen.

36. George Fox established the _____ movement.

   a. Pietist
   b. Anglican
   c. Quietist
   d. Quaker

37. The composer who dominated the German Protestant music was

   a. Ludwig van Beethoven.
   b. Johann Sebastian Bach.
   c. Wolfgang Amadeus Mozart.
   d. Franz Joseph Haydn.

38. The clergyman who has been called America's "greatest" theologian was

   a. Joseph Bellamy.
   b. Samuel Hopkins.
   c. Nathanel Emmons.
   d. Jonathan Edwards.

39. The great composer of Biblical oratorios in English was

   a. Johann Sebastian Bach.
   b. Antonio Vivaldi.
   c. George Frederick Handel.
   d. Ludwig van Beethoven.

40. Methodists were nurtured through an organization called the

   a. "Yoke-fellows."
   b. "Society."
   c. "Mission."
   d. "Club."

41. The English evangelist who befriended Benjamin Franklin during the Great Awakening was

   a. George Whitefield.
   b. Theordore Frelinghuysen.

    c. John Wesley.

    d. Charles Finney.

42. The British politician who devoted his career to the abolition of slave trading was

    a. William Pitt.

    b. William Wilberforce.

    c. Benjamin Disraeli.

    d. William Gladstone.

43. The American revivalist who stirred evangelical sentiment against slavery in the United States was

    a. George Whitefield.

    b. William Booth.

    c. Charles Finney.

    d. Francis Asbury.

44. The pastor of Victorian England's Metropolitan Tabernacle was

    a. D. L. Moody.

    b. George Muller.

    c. B. B. Warfield.

    d. Charles Spurgeon.

45. The reputation of _____ was established when he and Ira Sankey led successful revivals in Great Britain.

    a. Billy Sunday

    b. D. L. Moody

    c. Lyman Beecher

    d. none of the above

46. The term *neo-orthodoxy* is associated with

    a. R. A. Torrey.

    b. Louis Meyer.

    c. Karl Barth.

    d. James Orr.

47. The theologian who was associated with the plot to assassinate Hitler was

a. Baron von Trapp.
b. Harvey Cox.
c. Corrie ten Boom.
d. Dietrich Bonhoeffer.

48. The best-selling Christian author of all time is

a. Billy Graham.
b. John Bunyan.
c. C. S. Lewis.
d. Clement Moore.

49. The ministry of _____ is centered around L'Abri.

a. Francis Schaeffer.
b. Oswald Chambers.
c. John Mott.
d. A. W. Tozer.

50. The statement "The Bible says . . ." is repeatedly used by

a. Luis Palau.
b. Billy Sunday.
c. Pope John Paul II.
d. Billy Graham.

Answers

1. (d.) Polycarp (c. 70–156), a student under the Apostle John, was the beloved bishop of Smyrna. Persecution broke out in 156, and the eighty-six-year-old bishop was burned at the stake. Grief-stricken, his congregation began the custom of celebrating his death. Innocent memorials like this led to the later practice of "saint" worship, especially of martyrs.

2. (a.) The courage of the martyrs attracted the well-educated Gentile, Justin (c.100–165) to Christianity. As an apologist, Justin wrote *Dialogues*, a defense of the faith, in which he "conversed" with the Jew Trypho about Christianity. Around 155 Justin pleaded with Emperor Antonius Pius and his son,

Marcus Aurelius, for state toleration toward Christians. Ten years later Marcus Aurelius made Justin a martyr.

3. (c.) Irenaeus (c. 130–200), who sat under Polycarp in Smyrna as a child, became an anti-Gnostic polemicist in Lyons, France. Irenaeus countered Gnosticism with teachings from the early canon of the New Testament and promoted apostolic succession to offset the Gnostic belief that some apostles divulged a "secret tradition" to selected disciples.

4. (d.) Tertullian (c. 150–212) was the first Christian writer to use Latin, the language of the Roman Empire. The scope of his prolific writings classifies him as both an apologist and a polemicist and reveals the concerns of early church leaders about doctrine, theology, pastoring, and combating heresy.

5. (b.) Among the six thousand writings of Origen (c. 185–254) are two exceptional works. *First Principles* systematized theology, including sections on God, Christ, the Holy Spirit, creation, and the role of Scripture. *Hexapla*, an exegete's delight, is a book of six columns containing identical parallel texts in Hebrew, the Septuagint, and four other Greek versions.

6. (a.) Eusebius (c. 263–339) wrote a history of the church from the apostolic era to Constantine, which included valuable quotes from Christians whose work was later destroyed. His church history recorded Polycarp's trial, biographical sketches of leaders, and prevailing heresies, and Constantine's famous "cross in the sky" conversion. He also attended the Nicea Council.

7. (b.) Jerome (c. 331–420) was a Bible scholar who studied with the Eastern theologian Gregory of Nazianzus in Constantinople, served as secretary to Pope Damascus in Rome, and experimented with monasticism. His studies, travels, and monastic interests prepared him for the rigors of Bible translation. Jerome's Latin Vulgate took twenty-three years to prepare and was a masterpiece of scholarship.

8. (a.) John Chrysostom (c. 350–407), the "golden mouth," was an expository preacher. His eloquence earned him the office of bishop of Constantinople, one of the most prestigious positions in the empire. The people loved John, but Empress Eudoxia loathed his forthrightness and "arranged" his exile.

9. (c.) The *Confessions of Augustine* (c. 354–430), a classic in Christian literature, chronicles his spiritual and moral struggles. Theologically, Augustine's church doctrine ties him to Catholicism, but his doctrines of sin and grace link him with Protestantism. Augustine accepted the Apocrypha and promoted infant baptism.

10. (d.) Leo the Great (c.390–461) gave added status to the word *pope* which had been used to identify the bishops of major churches since the third century. Leo developed the idea that Christ was fully God and fully man, a teaching pronounced doctrine at the important Council of Chalcedon (451). Politically, Leo protected Rome from Attila, although he was not as successful with later barbarians.

11. (a.) The famous "Saint" Patrick (c. 389–461) was neither Irish nor Catholic! Born in Roman Britain, he was kidnapped as a youth and sent to work in Ireland. Patrick escaped, finished his education, and became a Celtic missionary. He set up a monastery and acted as a mediator among the local (usually warring) tribes. His spiritual adversaries were the Druids.

12. (b.) Columba (521–597) first established Celtic monasteries in his native Ireland. At age forty-two he moved to an island, Iona, and became a missionary to Scotland. Columba inspired a love for Bible study, an interest in music and Biblical poetry, and a Celtic zeal for evangelism. Other Celtic missionaries evangelized central and northern Europe.

13. (c.) Gregory the Great (c. 540–604) was the first medieval pope, the first pope to arise from monasticism, and the first pope to evangelize the English. He wielded power throughout the Mediterranean region. He simplified doctrine, which enabled the church to assimilate the barbarians more easily, and wrote a manual for training clergy that became the standard for the Middle Ages. Doctrinally, he promoted the concept of purgatory and encouraged the veneration of relics and images.

14. (d.) Bede (c. 672–735) spent his life in Britain's monastic libraries. His studies included Scripture, history, geography, hymnology, and grammar. His *Ecclesiastical History* traces the development of the English people from their earliest ties with Rome to 731 A.D.

15. (b.) While the Roman Church was reeling from its losses to Islam, Boniface (c. 672–754), an Anglo-Saxon missionary, sought papal permission to evangelize Germany. Boniface established monasteries, which became great centers of learning, and linked the pope to the French and German monarchies, thereby expanding European Christendom.

16. (a.) Alcuin (c. 735–804) worked with Charlemagne to Christianize Western Europe. He educated the royal family, the court, and the clergy, and stocked Charlemagne's library. He established the public school concept and required parishes to teach the Lord's Prayer and the Ten Commandments. Thank Alcuin, if you had to study Latin, the language he decreed all educated people should learn!

17. (d.) Bernard of Clairvaux (1090–1153) organized the Second Crusade and inspired militant monastic orders, such as the Knights Templar. Militant monastics were often brutal in their "defense" of the faith, the church, and Christians in the Holy Land. Their tradition of awarding crosses for military valor is still practiced in Britain and the United States.

18. (c.) Seeking control over the Church, King Henry II made his former chancellor Thomas à Becket (1118–1170) the archbishop of Canterbury. Once installed, however, Becket favored the church, particularly in the issue of jurisdiction over clergy convicted of crimes. Becket was exiled. Upon his return to England, Henry's knights murdered him in Canterbury Cathedral. The act enraged Christendom because churches were considered sanctuaries. Becket's shrine became the most popular destination for pilgrims in England.

19. (b.) Pope Innocent III (1160–1216) was a diplomat and an administrator who wielded power in Europe and the Eastern Church. He wrote more than five thousand letters and even tried to convert the Muslim king of Morocco via correspondence! His Twelfth Lateran Council issued landmark decisions: increasing papal authority, dogmatizing transubstantiation, requiring confession once a year, and confining Jews to ghettos.

20. (a.) The poverty vow of Francis of Assisi (1181–1228) irritated his wealthy father, but Francis believed possessions came between man and God. The Franciscans, sanctioned by

Innocent III in 1210, were friars who cared for the poor and the sick. After Francis' death, his widespread veneration greatly irritated the Reformers.

21. (b.) Thomas Aquinas (c. 1225–1274) was the greatest theologian of his day. He was large and gentle and nicknamed "the dumb ox," but writing and debate revealed his brilliant mind. Aquinas provided a framework for Christian thought which accommodated reason and revelation. The pivotal Council of Trent (1546) relied heavily on Aquinas' writings. In 1879 Pope Leo XIII declared his theology eternally valid.

22. (d.) John Wycliffe (c. 1329–1384) wanted reform. The Oxford philosopher espoused strong anticlerical views which John of Gaunt, the power behind the English throne, used to dilute ecclesiastical authority. Wycliffe's attack on major doctrines, e.g., the role of the Bible, transubstantiation, and papal authority, however, led to his dismissal from Oxford. His followers (the Lollards) issued a primitive English translation of the Bible in his name.

23. (c.) During the fourteenth century, church reform was a national movement in Bohemia. John Hus (1374–1415), a priest influenced by Wycliffe, believed that no one should establish teaching contrary to Scripture and spoke against the sale of indulgences, image worship, and pilgrimages. He was martyred for his "heretical" views which greatly influenced Luther.

24. (c.) Thomas à Kempis (1380–1471) is generally acknowledged to be the author of *Imitation of Christ*, one of the most widely read books in the world. The devotional is Christ-centered and simple in format.

25. (a.) At Castle Church, Martin Luther (1483–1546) began a lengthy, public examination of four basic issues: the nature of salvation, the seat of religious authority, the role of the church, and the response of the believer. The differing conclusions reached by the Reformers and the Roman Church forever altered Christian tradition.

26. (d.) Ulrich Zwingli (1484–1531), the Swiss reformer whose name sounds like a health food cereal, was a people's priest in Zurich. Like Luther, Zwingli's zeal for reform was the result of intensive, personal Bible study. Zwingli tenaciously up-

held the authority of Scripture, favored expository preaching, and promoted education.

27. (c.) Albrecht Dürer's (1471–1528) skill with woodcuts and copper engravings has never been equaled. His *Apocalypse*, a series of fifteen woodcuts depicting scenes from the book of Revelation, is breath-takingly detailed. Dürer painted portraits of Erasmus, Frederick the Wise (Luther's protector), and Melanchthon (Luther's successor). Dürer's *Hands* (a drawing of praying hands) is widely reproduced today.

28. (b.) William Tyndale (c. 1490–1536) was shocked by Biblical illiteracy, especially in the universities, where "no man shall look on the Scripture until he be noselled in heathen learning eight or nine years, and armed with false principles with which he is clean shut out of the understanding of the Scripture." For translating the Bible into English, Tyndale was executed in 1536; by 1539 English churches had the Bible whose New Testament was based on Tyndale's translation.

29. (a.) The Protestant Reformation prompted Ignatius Loyola (c. 1491–1556) to recommit his life to the pope and the Roman Church. Loyola, the "general" of the Jesuits, was one of the leading figures of the Catholic Counter Reformation.

30. (a.) As a result of personal Bible study, Menno Simons (1496–1561), an itinerant priest, formulated the distinctives of the Dutch Anabaptist movement: personal conversion, believer's (not infant's) baptism, and a Biblical lifestyle change. These Anabaptists were the forerunners of the modern Mennonites, Baptists, and Brethren.

31. (b.) John Calvin (1509–1564) is one of the most influential men in church history. In Geneva, Calvin demonstrated pastoral leadership, protected religious refugees, and provided a model community which students sought to emulate elsewhere. His *Institutes of the Christian Religion* defined Protestantism and lay the groundwork for democracy. His wisdom guided many Reformers, such as George Whitefield and Jonathan Edwards.

32. (c.) Scotland's John Knox (c. 1514–1572) led a colorful life as a Catholic priest, Anglican minister, bodyguard, galley slave, and exile in Calvin's Geneva. When Knox returned to

Scotland in 1559, his activities sparked the Scottish Reformation and his writings consolidated the movement.

33. (c.) John Foxe (1516–1587), a Protestant historian, published his famous book in exile. He later became a staunch supporter of Queen Elizabeth, who referred to him as "Our Father Foxe." The *Book of Martyrs* chronicles Christian persecution and reflects Foxe's belief that the Church of England was responsible for the world's destiny. This belief shaped British policy well into the twentieth century.

34. (b.) The brilliant Blaise Pascal (1623–1662) was profoundly influenced by Jansenism, a Catholic, anti-Jesuit movement based on Augustine's theology and a strict moral code. Pascal, who longed to write an apology for French atheists, died before he could begin the project, but his one-thousand "notes" published as *Pensées* reveal his deep spirituality.

35. (a.) Although he wrote nearly fifty other pieces, John Bunyan (1628–1688) is best known for *Pilgrim's Progress*, an allegory of the Christian life.

36. (d.) During the English Civil War, George Fox (1624–1691) founded the Quakers, pacifists who opposed slavery, promoted jail reform, and pressed for integrity in business. Because of their outspoken criticism of institutional churches, Quakers spent a lot of time in jail. Many fled to the American colonies, where they found refuge with William Penn. Today Quakers are mainly located in Kenya and the United States.

37. (b.) Bach (1685–1750), the great organ composer, was born in Eisenach, the city where Luther translated the Bible into German and wrote hymns. As an act of worship, Bach composed for the seasons of the church year. Among his outstanding pieces are his *Saint John* and *Saint Matthew Passions*.

38. (d.) Some theologians theorize in isolation, but Jonathan Edwards (1703–1758) wrote from the experiences of the Great Awakening. He also defended Christianity against Arminianism and deism, both of which, he said, "distanced" God.

39. (c.) The career of George Frederick Handel (1685–1759), Bach's contemporary, blossomed in England. Handel composed to present a strong Biblical message, as heard in his oratorios *The Messiah* and *Israel in Egypt*. Handel loved Biblical

poetry and the work of the Puritan John Milton. With Charles Wesley, Handel wrote "Rejoice, the Lord is King."

40. (b.) Although the Wesley brothers, John (1703–1791) and Charles (1707–1788), tried their hands at foreign missions in the American colony of Georgia, England became their mission field and factory workers, not Indians, their converts. Methodists were organized into societies arranged in geographical circuits and tended by the Wesleys or their assistants.

41. (a.) Although the Wesleys were not particularly influential in American missions, their friend George Whitefield (1714–1770), was. His often repeated "Ye must be born again!" convicted audiences on both sides of the Atlantic. Whitefield, estimated to have delivered thirty thousand sermons in his lifetime, worked unselfishly with all evangelicals whether they were Presbyterian, Baptist, Congregationalist, or Methodist.

42. (b.) John Newton, the slave trader turned hymn writer, counseled William Wilberforce (1759–1833) to champion the abolition of slave trading. Wilberforce, leader of the Clapham Sect, worked twenty years before the House of Commons abolished slave trading in England in 1807, the same year the United States abolished its slave trading. The House of Commons did not abolish the practice empirewide until 1833, just a few days before Wilberforce's death.

43. (c.) Whether writing or preaching, Charles Finney (1792–1875) espoused the authority of the Bible, the need for conversion, and Christian involvement in the world. In Finney's day, "involvement" meant fighting against slavery.

44. (d.) Charles Spurgeon (1834–1892), a simple country minister, became an English tourist attraction. Preaching at a time when Darwinism and liberal theology were on the rise, Spurgeon offered orthodoxy. From 1856 to 1917 (twenty-five years after his death), Spurgeon's sermons were published weekly. Apart from his preaching, his greatest work was a commentary on the Psalms titled *The Treasury of David.*

45. (b.) D. L. Moody (1837–1899), the unpolished, never ordained, shoe store salesman, invested his life in Christianity's "next generation." Whether he was witnessing to children in the slums of Chicago (where he was known as "Crazy Moody"), campaigning in England (where his work led to the conversion

of the "Cambridge Seven"), or establishing schools like Moody Bible Institute, Moody sought to prepare Christians for their future.

46. (c.) Neo-orthodoxy (which means a new way of looking at old doctrines) is associated with Swiss theologian Karl Barth (1886–1968). Barth, however, rejected the neo-orthodox label, because he did not agree with some of its other theologians (Bultmann, Bruner, and Tillich). Barth, neither conservative nor liberal, pulled Christian thought back from the emptiness of liberalism.

47. (d.) Although he was not involved in the attempt on Hitler's life, Dietrich Bonhoeffer (1906–1945) had known about the conspiracy and Hitler executed him in 1945. Bonhoeffer's life and writings, particularly *The Cost of Discipleship*, challenged the meaning of Christian commitment.

48. (c.) C. S. (Clive Staples) Lewis (1898–1963), might best be described as a literary evangelist. Lewis prepared unbelievers for Christianity with imaginative fiction, e.g., the *Chronicles of Narnia* and *Out of the Silent Planet*. Lewis also challenged believers with his nonfiction, personal letters, and two autobiographical novels. Forty million copies of his books have been sold worldwide.

49. (a.) After World War II, prevailing liberalism led Francis Schaeffer (1912–1984) to reexamine his beliefs about historical Chrisitianity. His own spiritual struggles led him to establish L'Abri, a faith ministry in Switzerland, which sheltered young people facing similar spiritual struggles. Schaeffer taught and counseled and emphasized the "Lordship of Christ in the totality of life." His later years were spent developing films (*Whatever Happened to the Human Race?*) and motivating discussion and Christian involvement in issues like abortion, civil rights, and euthanasia.

50. (d.) For fifty years, the message of Billy Graham (1918–), the unofficial leader of contemporary evangelicalism, has been: "The Bible says . . . ." Graham's bold, Biblical gospel has been presented in mass "crusades," on radio (the "Hour of Decision") and television, and in films and magazines. He co-founded *Christianity Today* and is the most widely recognized evangelist in history.

TWELVE

MODERN MISSIONS AND MISSIONARIES

"I NEED A BOOK, A GIFT FOR A FRIEND."

"Any particular subject?"

"No. But, I'd like something encouraging."

The clerk hesitated, then called out a title.

"I don't think so," came the response.

For the next few minutes a barrage of titles filled the air, followed by a round of no's. Then, there was an uneasy lull.

The shopper deliberated, then brightened. "Maybe a biography . . . "

"Good," said the clerk, her face a mixture of relief and inspiration. "I have something special. It just came in."

She slid a thick book onto the counter. On the glossy jacket was a portrait of a young woman from a bygone era and the title *A Chance to Die: The Life and Legacy of Amy Carmichael.*

"Who's Amy Carmichael?"

"Oh, she was an Irish missionary to India."

"Missionary? Oh, I don't want a missionary book! They're always so full of . . . pain."

The book buyer is not alone. Many of us turn away from missions and missionaries. Perhaps our world, too, is full of pain. Or, we're too busy. Or, we don't know any missionaries and missions seem remote. Whatever the reason, missions and missionaries are often treated like seasonal decorations—displayed at certain times in the church year and then put away.

That's too bad . . . for us. The history of missions discloses the power of the Holy Spirit, and it is a history worth celebrating.

As participants in the gospel of Jesus Christ, missionaries are our kindred spirits. Like us, they feel concern for the eternal welfare of others. Unlike us, they re-root their lives to demonstrate that concern.

The foreign missionary works at living. He twists his tongue around the awkward sounds of language. He dances hesitantly through the clumsy steps of culture. He dodges disease. Like Alice, he lives in a Wonderland, a world in which he never truly becomes a part.

A missionary rarely struggles with sharing the gospel. His battles are language, culture, relationships, illness, and isolation. Battles produce pain. The history of missions is a chronicle of pain: physical, emotional, and spiritual.

Missionaries like Paul understood physical pain, but so have others. Betty Olsen, a missionary nurse caught in the Tet offensive, marched twelve hours a day for eight months, enduring fever, malnutrition, beatings, and dysentery before her death at the hands of the Viet Cong. Adoniram Judson buried two wives. Illness plagued David Brainerd.

Other missionaries fought emotional battles. Ida Scudder long remembered her adolescence and the traumatic night her mother left her in Chicago to return to missionary work in India. Hudson Taylor grieved when bickering persisted among his missionary staff. China haunted C.T. Studd: "For five years we never went outside our doors without a volley of curses from our neighbors."

For others, spiritual responsibility caused pain. After seven arduous years in Bengal, William Carey had no Indian converts. Depression dogged A.B. Simpson, who was troubled by the "burden of a Christless world." Restlessness plagued Joy Ridderhof, who knew there was no "voice" for Christ in Honduras.

Survey the missionary movement and you'll surely find pain. But there's more to missions than pain.

In his old age, Pierre Auguste Renoir, the great French painter, was plagued by arthritis which twisted his fingers and hands. His friend and fellow artist, Henri Matisse, watched while Renoir carefully clasped a brush and painted in spite of the agony.

"Why persist?" pleaded Matisse. "The pain is too much."

Renoir shook his head. "The pain passes, but the beauty remains."

That's exactly what happens to the missionary movement. In spite of dysentery, death, squabbles, language, separation, and ridicule—in spite of the frailty of human beings—the gospel of Jesus Christ has reached into the corners of the world. And it persists. And the beauty remains. Those facts alone should encourage us to look into the lives of the missionaries and celebrate!

Questions

1. World evangelism began with

   a. the Reformation (1517).
   b. the Muslim capture of Jerusalem (642).
   c. the Roman and Byzantine church split (1054).
   d. Marco Polo's travels to China (c. 1271-1285).

2. Accompanying the Spanish and Portuguese explorers were members of the

   a. Church of England.
   b. Lutherans.
   c. Roman Catholic Church.
   d. Eastern Orthodox Church.

3. The "Apostle to the Indies and Japan," the most celebrated Jesuit missionary of all time,

   a. Matthew Ricci.
   b. Francis Xavier.
   c. Ignatius Loyola.
   d. Jacques Marquette.

4. "Planted" in the New England colonies during the seventeenth century were _____ who propagated their faith.

   a. Anglicans
   b. Franciscans
   c. Jesuits
   d. Pilgrims and Puritans

5. Missions were established in Canada in the seventeenth century by

   a. France.
   b. Italy.
   c. Spain.
   d. Portugal.

6. The nobleman who founded Herrnhut, the Moravian religious community which supplied missionaries to North and South America, the Virgin Islands, Greenland, and South Africa by 1740, was

   a. Francis Xavier.
   b. King Frederick IV.
   c. Count Nicolaus Ludwig von Zinzendorf.
   d. Ludwig von Beethoven.

7. The statement which describes the Moravian missionary emphasis is:

   a. minister with medicine.
   b. every Christian, regardless of education, is a missionary and should witness as he practices his trade.
   c. convert the intellectuals and the masses will follow.
   d. introduce commerce and Christianity will follow.

8. The English colonies in America that most faithfully pursued evangelism among the Indians were

   a. the Mid-southern colonies.
   b. the Western colonies.
   c. the Southern colonies.
   d. the New England colonies.

9. The missionary to the Indians who was befriended by Jonathan Edwards and betrothed to his daughter, whose writings influenced countless missionaries, was

   a. Eleazer Wheelock.
   b. David Brainerd.
   c. Charles Wesley.
   d. David Zeisberger.

10. The "Father of Modern Missions" was

    a. Adoniram Judson.
    b. William Carey.
    c. Francis Xavier.
    d. Count Nicolaus von Zinzendorf.

11. The organization that provided early Protestant missionaries with direction, support, and purpose was

    a. the Mission society.
    b. the East India Trade Company.
    c. Lloyds of London.
    d. the Bible institute.

12. Protestant evangelism during the nineteenth century was greatly aided by

    a. government subsidies.
    b. benign living conditions.
    c. dedicated Bible societies.
    d. all of the above.

13. Among America's first foreign missionaries in 1812 were

    a. Adoniram and Nancy Judson.
    b. David and Mary Livingstone.
    c. John and Mary Moffat.
    d. William and Dorothy Carey.

14. Missionary endeavors in China and India were thwarted by

    a. the Red Cross.
    b. Lloyds of London.

    c. the U.S. State Department.

    d. the East India Company.

15. Henry Martyn translated the New Testament into Hindustani, Persian, and Arabic while he was employed as a

    a. ship builder.

    b. chaplain for the East India Company.

    c. manager of a tea plantation.

    d. musician.

16. Robert Morrison is best known for his work in China as a

    a. doctor.

    b. newspaper journalist.

    c. disaster/relief organizer.

    d. Bible translator and author of a dictionary.

17. The "White Man's Graveyard" is in

    a. South America.

    b. China.

    c. Africa.

    d. Greenland.

18. The "Missionary Patriarch of South Africa" was

    a. David Livingstone.

    b. John Moffat.

    c. Patrick Hamilton.

    d. Charles Mackay.

19. The statement which best describes David Livingstone's contribution to the missionary movement is:

    a. He translated the Bible into scores of native languages.

    b. He established schools for native converts.

    c. He successfully combined missionary and family life.

    d. He charted Africa's interior for other missionaries to settle.

20. The writings of this reporter inspired international support for African missions:

    a. George Grenfell.
    b. Alexander Mackay.
    c. Mary Slessor.
    d. Henry Stanley.

21. Historically, attempts to evangelize China were thwarted by

    a. China's policy of isolationism.
    b. internal wars.
    c. language barriers.
    d. unsanitary living conditions.

22. Jonathan and Rosalind Goforth, Canadian missionaries to China, presented the gospel before they conducted tours of

    a. the Imperial Palace.
    b. a Canadian ship.
    c. their home.
    d. a Chinese restaurant.

23. During the 19th century, missionary work among the American Indians diminished because of

    a. conflict over control of the land.
    b. an increased emphasis on foreign missions.
    c. native interference with the advance of American society.
    d. all of the above.

24. The "Haystack Prayer Meeting" led several American college students to commit their lives to missions and also led to

    a. U.S. government support for overseas mission work.
    b. the first U.S. foreign mission board.
    c. an evangelistic thrust in Latin America.
    d. cooperation between Western and Third World missionaries.

25. In 1795 the London Missionary Society (LMS) was established to send missionaries to the South Pacific. The English explorer instrumental in its formation was which of the following:

    a. Henry Hudson.
    b. Ferdinand Magellan.
    c. Christopher Columbus.
    d. Captain James Cook.

26. The person *not* a missionary in the South Pacific was

    a. C. I. Scofield.
    b. John Williams.
    c. John G. Paton.
    d. John Geddie.

27. The outspoken Southern Baptist missionary to China who urged U.S. women to support foreign missions was

    a. T. P. Crawford.
    b. Lottie Moon.
    c. Annie Armstrong.
    d. Edmonia Moon.

28. Colonialist and imperialist attitudes led many nineteenth-century missionaries to equate Christianity with

    a. Western civilization.
    b. political revolution.
    c. national self-determination.
    d. intellectualism.

29. Amy Carmichael's Dohnavur Fellowship ministered to

    a. lepers.
    b. the aged.
    c. children.
    d. families in foreign service.

30. "England's greatest cricketer," the wealthy and brilliant man who gave away his fortune in order to become a student volunteer missionary, was

   a. William Cameron Townsend.
   b. Fletcher Brockman.
   c. E. Stanley Jones.
   d. C. T. Studd.

31. The *untrue* phrase about the Student Volunteer Movement (1886–1936) is:

   a. staffed by intelligent young men who gave up personal wealth, position, and prestige for missions.
   b. excluded China and India as target mission fields.
   c. formed a cooperative, interdenominational team.
   d. encouraged and nurtured by Dwight L. Moody.

32. The China Inland Mission (CIM) gave birth to the

   a. Faith Mission Movement.
   b. Student Volunteer Movement.
   c. mission societies.
   d. all of the above.

33. A strict requirement for the CIM missionaries was

   a. marriage.
   b. advanced theological training.
   c. service without furloughs.
   d. chinese style of dress.

34. Raymond Lull, Samuel Zwemer, and William Borden evangelized

   a. Buddhists.
   b. Taoists.
   c. Muslims.
   d. Hindus.

35. The Faith Missionary Movement was characterized by:

   a. no guaranteed, set income for its missionaries.

b. conservative evangelicalism.
c. Bible institute and Christian college volunteers.
d. all of the above.

36. The "Great Century" for the global spread of Protestant Christianity was the

a. tenth century.
b. sixteenth century.
c. nineteenth century.
d. twentieth century.

37. During the first half of the twentieth century, the focal point for world-wide mission endeavors shifted from England to

a. Australia.
b. New Zealand.
c. Canada.
d. America.

38. Claiming the most lives of Protestant missionaries was

a. the Boxer rebellion.
b. the New Tribes murders.
c. the Mau Mau rebellion.
d. the Waiilatpu massacre.

39. By 1910, women missionaries outnumbered men because

a. men were barred from service by foreign governments.
b. single women were accepted as missionaries.
c. disease diminished the ranks of men.
d. none of the above.

40. One major geographical area overlooked by Protestant missionaries until the late nineteenth/early twentieth century was

a. South Africa.
b. French Polynesia.
c. Latin America.
d. East Africa.

41. During the 1930s, Clarence Jones and the "Voice of the Andes" spread the gospel in Ecuador using

    a. tape recorders.
    b. Bible correspondence courses.
    c. air-dropped tracts.
    d. radio programs.

42. Ida Scudder, Albert Schweitzer, Helen Roseveare, Carl Becker, and Viggo Olsen were "missionary specialists" in

    a. medicine.
    b. agriculture.
    c. education.
    d. linguistics.

43. By 1950 the region considered a "new" mission field was

    a. the South Pacific.
    b. Europe.
    c. North Africa.
    d. India.

44. In January 1956, Nate Saint, Jim Elliot, Pete Fleming, Ed McCully, and Roger Youderian were murdered in a daring attempt to evangelize

    a. North African Muslims.
    b. Panamanian officials.
    c. South American Indians.
    d. Haitian hurricane victims.

45. The Summer Institute of Linguistics (SIL) is most closely associated with

    a. the Moody Bible Institute.
    b. the YMCA.
    c. the Wycliffe Bible Translators.
    d. World Vision.

46. The chronological advance William Cameron Townsend utilized in evangelism was

   a. radio.
   b. aviation.
   c. linguistics.
   d. all of the above.

47. In 1989 one out of every ten missionaries from North American was a graduate of

   a. Wheaton College.
   b. Moody Bible Institute.
   c. Bible Institute of Pennsylvania.
   d. Nyack College.

48. "Redemptive Analogy," the application of spiritual truth to native customs, challenged missionaries in cross-cultural situations. It was introduced by

   a. Brother Andrew.
   b. Bob Pierce.
   c. Luis Palau.
   d. Don Richardson.

49. A missiologist is a

   a. trained professional who studies mission strategies.
   b. person who prepares primers for unwritten languages.
   c. missionary with a secondary, technological skill.
   d. liaison between the missionary and his sponsor.

50. The gospel message of the modern missionary is:

   a. Jesus offers health, wealth, and prosperity.
   b. Christianity raises all standards of living.
   c. Christianity cures social injustice.
   d. Jesus died for your sins.

Answers

1. (a.) Although there had been missionary efforts throughout the Middle Ages, interest in global evangelization exploded

during the Reformation. The interest was prompted by the land "discoveries" of the fifteenth- and sixteenth-century explorers.

2. (c.) King Ferdinand of Spain ordered Catholic missionaries to accompany explorers after Columbus's first voyage to the New World. Portugal followed suit. Five years after Luther posted his theses, the Spanish had missions in Cuba. By the American Revolution, Catholic missions—Dominican, Franciscan, Augustinian, and Jesuit—were established in Florida, Texas, California, Mexico, Central and South America, the Philippines, Africa, the East Indies, and the Orient.

3. (b.) The most celebrated Jesuit missionary of all time was Francis Xavier, a Spaniard of noble birth and a founding member of the Jesuits. Xavier worked in India, Indonesia, and Japan, and died in 1552 attempting to evangelize China.

4. (d.) Although not strictly classified as missionaries, the Pilgrims, who landed at Plymouth, and the Puritans, who settled Boston, were missionaries in deed. They propagated their faith and carried on humanitarian work (see answer 8).

5. (a.) France established the Quebec mission in 1608 and went on to explore the Mississippi Valley and Louisiana. Mission stations trailed the explorers. When the French were driven from North America, only the Jesuit missions in Quebec and Louisiana remained.

6. (c.) Count Zinzendorf, a contemporary of John Wesley and George Whitefield, was a pivotal figure in foreign missions. Zinzendorf opened his estate to religious refugees whose spiritual differences faded during a revival in 1727. From that point on, the Moravian community was committed to missions. Statistics project that Herrnhut commissioned more missionaries during its first two decades than all Protestant and Anglican churches had in the previous two centuries.

7. (b.) The Moravians were lay people, not theologians, skilled at a trade and trained in evangelism. Their trade provided missionary opportunities; they witnessed as they worked. Their message was the love and sacrifice of Christ for all men. Little emphasis was placed on doctrine. Their worship was emotional and somewhat mystic, a fact which sometimes troubled other Christian groups.

8. (d.) America's colonies were first settled by merchants, religious dissenters, and gentry. New England attracted the dissenters, the Pilgrims and the Puritans, who, in turn, evangelized the Indians. Among the New England pastors with outstandng Indian ministries were John Eliot, Thomas Mayhew, and Eleazer Wheelock.

9. (b.) American-born David Brainerd was another New Englander who worked among the Indians from 1742 until his death in 1747. Although Brainerd was intense, educated, and capable, his impulsive spirit often thrust him into situations illprepared. Brainerd's legacy to missions stems more from his personal observations, recorded in diaries and journals, than from innovative techniques or numerical success. Both William Carey and Henry Martyn were influenced by the honest, melancholy Brainerd.

10. (b.) William Carey is the "Father of Modern Missions." How an impoverished English shoemaker with enormous family responsibilities and a thimblefull of formal education developed the financial backing, the perseverance, and the ability to translate Scripture into three different Indian languages is nothing short of a miracle. Carey's concept of missions developed as he read the Bible, Captain Cook's *Voyages*, and the journals of David Brainerd.

Carey's goal in India was to develop a church staffed by well-trained natives, who were equipped with the Scriptures in their native tongues. Carey did not discard Indian culture, although he fought against the practices of burning widows and abandoning newborns. Carey's skills as a translator were not superlative. "I can plod." he wrote. "I can persevere in any definite pursuit. To this I owe everything." Carey plodded. He expected "great things from God." He attempted "great things for God," and his example inspired the missionaries of the nineteenth century.

11. (a.) When William Carey introduced the idea of foreign missions to a Baptist minister's association in 1793, the Baptists created an organization: the Mission Society. Other groups adopted the concept. Mission societies recruited volunteers and directed evangelistic efforts around the world. The societies,

staffed by laymen and not by clergy, were directly responsibile for making Christianity a major world religion.

12. (c.) Bible societies provided much needed Scripture texts and made missions a "team" effort. Missionaries acquired foreign translations; the societies published Bible texts without doctrinal comment; and local churches underwrote the distribution and cost.

13. (a.) Adoniram and Nancy Judson were among the eight missionaries first commissioned by the American Board of Commissioners for Foreign Missions in 1812, although the American Baptist Missionary Board later underwrote their support. The Judsons, who worked briefly in India, were deported by the East India Company before settling in Burma. Adoniram took twenty-six years to complete his translation of the Bible into the exceedingly complex Burmese language.

14. (d.) The East India Company regulated British trade. Since the early missionaries came from nontraditional groups (Carey from the Baptists, for instance), missionaries were considered radicals. For economic reasons, the East India Company did not want to offend the Muslims or the Hindus. Consequently, the East India Company closely regulated all missionary activity as well.

15. (b.) Henry Martyn was a chaplain hired to provide spiritual care for the employees and families of the East India Company in India. He met William Carey who quickly recognized and encouraged his talent for Bible translation. After five years in India, poor health forced Martyn to retreat to Persia, where he died at the age of thirty-one.

16. (d.) Robert Morrison produced a Chinese translation of the Bible. Morrison's work in China was closely monitored by the East India Company. All language studies initially were done in secret. When Morrison published a Chinese-English dictionary, the East India Company recognized his talents and hired him as a translator. Although Morrison was irritated by his association with the East India Company, his duties provided him with unusual language opportunities and greatly aided his translation of the Bible.

17. (c.) Africa, the "White Man's Graveyard," has claimed the lives of more Protestant missionaries than any other region.

The first American Methodist missionary, Melville B. Cox, arrived in Liberia in 1833 and died within four months. His story is not unusual. When Adlai Stevenson toured Africa during the 1960s, he was astounded by the number of missionary graves. Those determined to evangelize Africa faced indigenous disease: typhus, malaria, yellow fever, and dysentery.

18. (b.) John Moffat, the "Missionary Patriarch of South Africa," was one of the first missionaries to penetrate South Africa's interior and gain the respect of tribal leaders. Moffat, who believed in "the Bible and the plough," built a model missionary compound at Kuruman, where he taught Scripture and farming and trained native pastors and missionary apprentices. After fifty-three years in Africa (with only one furlough), Moffat and his wife retired to England.

19. (d.) David Livingstone, John Moffat's son-in-law, excelled as a pioneer/explorer who literally "mapped" Africa. The account of his first expedition, *Missionary Travels and Researches in South Africa*, earned him international fame.

20. (d.) The New York *Herald* sent Henry Stanley to "find David Livingstone," who by 1871 was an international figure. Stanley's contribution to missions came as a writer who pleaded for volunteers: "Oh, that some pious, practical missionary would come here!"

21. (a.) Although there had been intermittent attempts to evangelize China, the Chinese fear of foreigners dictated a strict policy of isolationism. In the nineteenth century, mission opportunities centered around Canton and Macao, the ports open to foreign residents. Missionaries were rebuffed by the Chinese who resented the East India Company for illegally smuggling opium into China. To the Chinese, the missionary and the trader were both "foreign devils."

22. (c.) In 1888 Jonathan and Rosalind Goforth used their home with its Western interior design and its "modern" furnishings (a sewing machine, a stove, and an organ) to attract thousands of Chinese. Jonathan conducted house tours and presented the gospel, while Rosalind met with the women in the yard. When Jonathan later began an itinerant ministry, many of those who came to hear him had been "guests" in the Goforth home.

23. (d.) Indian evangelism decreased as pioneers struggled for supremacy of the land and moved westward. During the nineteenth century, foreign missions, not Indian missions, attracted aspiring missionaries.

24. (b.) The "Haystack Prayer Meeting," a manifestation of the Second Great Awakening, led to formation of the American Board of Commissioners for Foreign Missions in 1810. The board supported the missions decisions made by several college students. Among those first commissioned by the board were Adoniram Judson and Luther Rice.

25. (d.) *The Last Voyages of Captain Cook* spurred Protestants to form the London Missionary Society with its "fundamental principle that our design is not to send Presbyterianism, Independency, Episcopacy or any other form of church government . . . but the glorious gospel of the blessed God to the heathen."

26. (a.) C. I. Scofield founded the Central American Mission and was not associated with the South Pacific. John Williams, evangelized the islands near Tahiti. John Geddie and the dynamic John Paton preached, trained native workers, and translated Scriptures in the New Hebrides.

27. (b.) Lottie Moon inspired Southern Baptist women to become missionaries, to encourage a foreign missions emphasis at home, and to contribute regularly to foreign missions. The annual Lottie Moon Christmas Offering is legendary.

28. (a.) The three C's—Christianity, commerce, and civilization—led many missionaries to equate Christianity with Western civilization. Some missionaries imposed Western culture on converts. Others protected their converts from commercial exploitation.

29. (c.) Amy Carmichael ministered to children, particularly girls, who had been sold for Hindu temple prostitution.

30. (d.) When C.T. Studd and six other sophisticated, talented Cambridge students pledged themselves to Chinese missions, the news stunned British society. Studd spent nearly ten years in China working with opium addicts before ill health forced him back to England. He then became a popular speaker for the Student Volunteer Movement in Europe and the United States. At the age of fifty, Studd began the Heart of Africa Mission to the Belgian Congo. Studd's methods, his in-

tense personality, and his vigorous lifestyle made him a controversial figure. Yet, his personal sacrifice and unyielding commitment to missions were exemplary.

31. (b.) The Student Volunteer Movement, a missions organization propelled by the vision of Robert Wilder, the dynamism of D. L. Moody, and the administration of John Mott, combed college campuses for student volunteers. The students were irresistibly drawn to China and India, and, because they were educated in fields other than theology, they gained easy access to the elite.

32. (a.) CIM set the pattern for the Faith Mission Movement and influenced at least forty other organizations, including the Christian and Missionary Alliance, the Evangelical Alliance Mission, and the Sudan Interior Mission. "Faith mission" was a term given to interdenominational organizations which did not have the financial backing of a specific church (see answer 35).

33. (d.) CIM missionaries were required to adopt a Chinese style of dress which was more suited to the climate and gave missionaries greater freedom among the Chinese.

34. (c.) Lull, Zwemer, and Borden evangelized the Muslims. Raymond Lull was a Franciscan apologist in North Africa during the Crusades. He was one of the few Christians who presented the gospel, not the sword, to the Muslims. Samuel Zwemer ministered in Arabia and Egypt from 1890 to 1929. William Borden was a "student volunteer" who worked with Zwemer in Cairo.

35. (d.) The Faith Missionary Movement guaranteed no set income, sprang from conservative evangelicalism, and was staffed by Bible institute and Christian college graduates.

36. (c.) The "Great Century" for Protestant evangelism was the nineteenth century. Missionary outreach was primarily a byproduct of the Great Awakenings.

37. (d.) During the first half of the twentieth century, America began to emerge as a world power. Europe, battered by wars, continued to send missionaries abroad, but leadership and innovation in missions shifted to the United States.

38. (a.) In June 1900, an imperial decree ordered the death of all foreigners and abolished Christianity in China. The resulting violence was called the Boxer rebellion in which 135

missionaries and 53 missionary children were murdered. Particularly hard hit was CIM, which lost 91 missionaries.

39. (b.) Women had long been a part of missions. During the nineteenth century, however, there was a reluctance to sponsor unmarried women on foreign fields. CIM was among the first mission agencies to accept single women. Missionary societies exclusively for women started in England and spread to the United States. By 1900 there were over forty agencies in America alone. As missionary programs began to emphasize teaching and medicine, women played an increasingly important role.

40. (c.) One of the last regions for Protestant evangelization was Latin America, where the Catholic Church had long been established. (The Catholic University of San Marcos in Lima was founded in 1551.) The United Methodists, the United Presbyterians, and the Southern Baptists made major commitments to the area late in the nineteenth century. One modern missionary who made astounding inroads was Ken Strachan of the Latin American Mission (LAM).

41. (d.) By 1930 the radio was a evangelistic tool in the United States. But Clarence Jones envisioned radio as an evangelistic tool in Catholic Ecuador, a nation which had only thirteen receivers. In spite of many setbacks, HCJB (Heralding Christ Jesus' Blessings) became the "Voice of the Andes" on Christmas Day 1931, using a 250-watt transmitter. All thirteen receivers were tuned in, and the station prospered. HCJB continues today as an outstanding example of Christian broadcasting.

42. (a.) These missionaries were specialists in medicine. The twentieth century missionary discovered that skill in technological areas, such as medicine, linguistics, and aviation, often provided unique opportunities for evangelism.

43. (b.) In the aftermath and disillusionment of two world wars, Europe became a mission field. Missionaries responded to the need in different ways. Paul Freed established Trans World Radio, aimed at Europe and the Mediterranean. Peter Deyneka supplied radio programs, particularly to Iron Curtain countries. Brother Andrew smuggled Bibles.

44. (c.) Although their fate was not known for several days, the five missionaries were murdered as they attempted to reach the Auca Indians of Ecuador. The incident attracted world-wide attention and was recorded in Elizabeth Elliot's book *Through Gates of Splendor.*

45. (c.) SIL is the sister organization of Wycliffe Bible Translators. SIL is a training program which equips prospective translators to handle the alphabet, grammar, idioms, etc., of foreign languages and to translate the Bible, teach literacy, and produce native language materials.

46. (d.) The innovative and sometimes controversial William Cameron Townsend made technology work for Christ. Radio kept missionaries in touch with home bases, aviation provided safe transportation and opportunities for surveillance in remote areas, and linguistics equipped missionaries to record unwritten languages. Billy Graham called Townsend "the greatest missionary of our time."

47. (b.) Moody Bible Institute is one of the outstanding training schools for missionaries today. Since 1890 over 5,800 Moody alumni have served under 255 mission boards in 108 countries of the world. Of this number, more than 2,300 were still active in 1981. Half of the missionary pilots in the world are graduates of the Moody Aviation program.

48. (d.) Don Richardson introduced Christians to his theory of "Redemptive Analogy" in the best-selling book *Peace Child.* The principle of "redemptive analogy" encourages language specialists to identify and draw upon themes from native folklore and customs that are similar to Biblical concepts.

49. (a.) A missiologist studies mission strategies. In the past only Bible colleges offered missions courses; in recent times seminaries have included missions in their curricula, some offering advanced degrees in missions and evangelism. Missiology, built around a vital concern for the twenty-first century, was given academic status in 1973 with the founding of the American Society of Missiology. Their publication, *Missiology: An International Review,* reports on the developing trends, techniques, and philosophies in Christian missions.

50. (d.) The gospel for the modern missionary is the gospel of the New Testament: Jesus died for your sins and for mine.

Christianity is not Biblical knowledge, doctrine, or a review of the heroes of the faith. Christianity is a relationship with Jesus Christ that changes lives.

If you have not personally accepted Jesus Christ as Lord and Savior, will you do it now? Simply bow your head, ask Jesus to forgive your sins, and invite Him to take control of your life. Then, commit some time each day to reading the Bible where you will begin to see life from God's perspective.

If you have invited Jesus into your life, you may not feel any different at this moment. In fact, you may feel alone. However, salvation is not based on feeling but on Who God is. The Bible says you are a member of the household of God (Ephesians 2:18–19). Jesus intercedes for you daily. The Holy Spirit guards your spiritual walk. I pray for you, too, "that you may be filled with the knowledge of His will in all spiritual wisdom and understanding, so that you may walk in a manner worthy of the Lord, to please Him in all respects, bearing fruit in every good work and increasing in the knowledge of God" (Colossians 1:9–10).

SUGGESTED READINGS

THE BEST SOURCE FOR IMPROVING YOUR CHRISTIAN LITERACY is the Bible—consistently and intelligently read. There is great benefit from reading Bible passages in different translations. If you have been reading the same translation of the Bible for decades, it is time to supplement your reading with a modern language translation.

For a general hands-on introduction or review of the Bible, read *30 Days to Understanding the Bible* by Dr. Max E. Anders (Brentwood, Tennessee, 1988). An investment of thirty minutes a day for thirty days will yield a basic understanding of the Bible, a grasp of essential doctrines, and an awareness of the principles of Christian living.

Color Thru the Bible (available from the Walk Thru the Bible Ministries, 61 Perimeter Park, N.E., P.O. Box 80587, Atlanta, Georgia 30366) is a delightful, visual teaching tool designed for children. Each book of the Old Testament is summarized by an appropriate, detailed illustration. Before passing the book on to a child, however, adults would do well to study the "portraits" of the prophets, particularly the minor prophets.

For a comprehensive study of church history, Eerdman's *The History of Christianity* (Grand Rapids, Michigan, 1987) is a classic. *Church History* by Howard F. Vos (Chicago, 1984) is a short, straightforward presentation of this complex subject.

Finally, two informative, easily obtained, and well-written books about the people of the post-New Testament era are: *From Jerusalem to Irian Jaya* by Ruth Tucker (Grand Rapids, Michigan, 1983) and *Great Leaders of the Christian Church* edited by John D. Woodbridge (Chicago: Moody Press, 1988).

ABOUT THE AUTHOR

JUDITH A. LUNSFORD taught literature, history, public speaking, and creative writing in secondary schools in Illinois, Alabama, and Georgia. She also worked for the Atomic Energy Commission at the Lawrence Radiation Laboratory in Berkeley, California.

After the birth of her son, she devoted her energies to teaching adult Sunday school classes, leading Bible studies, and conducting ladies' seminars. She has been a free-lance writer since 1986. *Test Your Christian Literacy* is her first book.

Mrs. Lunsford currently lives in Marietta, Georgia, with her husband, Gary, a physicist at Georgia Tech, and teenage son, Tobin. The family has two Golden Retrievers, Joshua ad Caleb.

The typeface for the text of this book is *Baskerville*. It's creator, John Baskerville (1706-1775), broke with tradition to reflect in his type the rounder, yet more sharply cut lettering of eighteenth-century stone inscriptions and copy books. The type foreshadows modern design in such novel characteristics as the increase in contrast between thick and thin strokes and the shifting of stress from the diagonal to the vertical strokes. Realizing that this new style of letter would be most effective if cleanly printed on smooth paper with genuinely black ink, he built his own presses, developed a method of hot pressing the printed sheet to a smooth, glossy finish, and experimented with special inks. However, Baskerville did not enter into general commercial use in England until 1923.

Substantive Editing:
Michael S. Hyatt

Copy Editing:
Alice Ewing

Cover Design:
Kent Puckett Associates, Atlanta, Georgia

Page Composition:
Xerox Ventura Publisher
Printware 720 IQ Laser Printer

Printing and Binding:
Ringier, America
Olathe, Kansas